W9-CIL-563

The Vietnam War Soldier Stories

Untold Tales of the Soldiers on the Battlefields of the Vietnam War

Third Edition

All Rights Reserved. No part of this publication may be reproduced in any form or by any means, including scanning, photocopying, or otherwise without prior written permission of the copyright holder. Copyright © 2015

Disclaimer Notice:

Please note the information contained within this document is for educational purposes only.

Every attempt has been made to provide accurate, up to date and reliable complete information no warranties of any kind are expressed or implied. Readers acknowledge that the author is not engaging in rendering legal, financial or professional advice.

By reading any document, the reader agrees that under no circumstances are we responsible for any losses, direct or indirect, which are incurred as a result of use of the information contained within this document, including – but not limited to errors, omissions, or inaccuracies.

Table of Contents

Introduction

Thank you for downloading this book, "The Vietnam War Soldier Stories: Untold Tales of Soldiers on the Battlefields of the Vietnam War".

*The Vietnam War conjures up many emotions, images, and events in different parts of the world. In Vietnam itself, the war for independence lasted for over a century. Becoming a colony of France in the late 1800's, many in Vietnam, then known in the West as "Annam" and part of "Indochina", fought for independence from France until 1940, when France ceded control of Vietnam and their other Southeast Asian possessions to Japan, an ally of Nazi Germany, which had just humiliatingly defeated the French in May/June 1940.

The struggle of the Vietnamese from foreign control continued during the Japanese occupation, and at times, Vietnamese resisters on both the left and the right of the political spectrum found themselves allied with the French, whose rule, while oppressive, was less so than that of the Japanese.

With victory over the Japanese in 1945, France, used to being a power that mattered in world affairs but no longer so after WWII, attempted to regain some of her prestige and territory. This resulted in the French re-occupying Vietnam, Laos and Cambodia. They then divided into three administrative sections, Tonkin China in the north, Annam in the center, and Cochin China in the south. In all of these countries, but most prominently in the north of Vietnam, the indigenous people fought back. This war, known as the "Indo-China War" in France, and the "Anti-French Resistance War" in Vietnam, ended in 1954 with independence of Tonkin China and the northern section of Annam, which became known as "North Vietnam."

The episode that sealed the French defeat in North Vietnam was the Battle of Dien Bien Phu in the highlands of western North Vietnam, which was a humiliating defeat of the French by Vietnamese forces led by General Vo Nguyen Giap (1911-2013). Assisting the French forces at Dien Bien Phu and other areas was the United States, which dropped supplies and arms to the besieged forces of the French. As an interesting side note: many of the troops fighting under the French flag were troops of the French Foreign Legion, mostly non-French volunteers who wished to erase their past by gaining French citizenship after their tour as Legionnaires was over. Others were WWII vets who could not make the transition to peacetime. A small number of those were ex-Waffen-SS soldiers, whom after being not so thoroughly vetted for war crimes during WWII, were now fighting for their enemy of 1940-45.

After the defeat of the French in the North, an international conference in Geneva partitioned the country into two parts. North of the 17th Parallel would be communist controlled North Vietnam, led by revolutionary leader and French educated Ho Chi Minh. South of the 17th Parallel, a regime set up under the nominal control of Emperor Bao Dai would rule "South Vietnam." The regime of Ho Chi Minh, while seeming to accept this arrangement, worked both covertly and overtly to overthrow the government of South Vietnam. France knew this, yet was unable to completely halt the effort of the North Vietnamese.

In the South, Bao Dai was the figurehead under an ever-changing military and rightist cabal. As the 1950's turned into the 1960's, the French, who population at home was increasingly against French involvement in Asia and elsewhere (notably North Africa/Algeria), and whose economy was suffering, asked the United States to back up and reinforce the regime in South Vietnam.

American involvement, which increased in the late 1950's and especially after the famous "Gulf of Tonkin Incident" of 1964, brought increased resentment in the North and much of the South, which believed the Americans were simply replacing the colonial rule of the French with their own. A renewed effort to unify the nation under the rule of the North Vietnamese communists therefore began once again to gain momentum. The Vietnamese call the battle against the Americans "The American War." The Vietnam War was arguably the first war lost by the United States, and resulted in the unification of Vietnam under the Vietnamese Communist Party.

For the Vietnamese, the departure of the USA from the area did not end the warfare that had been going on since the 19th century. In 1978, the Vietnamese invaded Cambodia, with the implied approval of the United States, to both end the genocide occurring there and to topple the extremely radical regime of Pol Pot, whose troops had been encroaching on Vietnamese territory. Reacting to this attack on their Cambodian ally, the Chinese who had traditionally been a foe of Vietnam, but an ally in the war against the USA and then an enemy once again, attacked North Vietnam, which resulted in a short but intense border war. By the end of this conflict, the Vietnamese had been at war in some way or another for over one hundred years.

Until 2011, the "Vietnam War", as it is called in the United States, was the longest conflict in American history. That distinction is now held by the war in Afghanistan, which began in 2001 and is still going on in 2015. By comparison, the Vietnam War was far more costly in terms of lives lost, both on the American and Vietnamese side. It was also far more costly in many ways, to American society, for the Vietnam War divided America like no other conflict has, with the exception of the Civil War in the 19th century.

The impact and aftereffects of the war are still being felt forty years after the last US troops left Vietnam. Vietnam veterans, now in their sixties and seventies, still make up a significant portion of the nations' homeless. The aftereffect of the war, in terms of wounds and psychological effects, still take their toll on veterans and their families.

An easy way to provoke an argument within a large family which includes people in their 50's-80's in the United States is to bring up the Vietnam War. The war toppled the Johnson Administration, divided American society and caused sometimes violent resistance to government action, caused widespread demoralization in the nations' military, and sowed much distrust between the government and the people of the United States. The Watergate scandal of 1972-74 might have also indirectly been caused by the Vietnam War. Richard Nixon, had been promising to end the war since his election in 1968. He felt that the election of George McGovern in 1972 would undermine Nixon's efforts to achieve "peace" took part in the break- in of Democratic and President Nixon himself in its subsequent cover-up, which eventually brought down his government and further angered and alienated the American people.

Ironically, the United States and the People's Republic of Vietnam today have relatively close relations and are frequently found acting in concert, at least diplomatically, in their common interests vis-a-vis China in southern Asia.

This e-book is meant to be an introduction to the Vietnam War and the men who fought in it. We hope that it encourages you to do further research on this fascinating period of history, the effects of which are still with us today.

Please feel free to share this book with your friends and family. Please also take the time to write a short review on Amazon to share your thoughts.

Chapter 1: Images

In many ways, the world saw the Vietnam War as it was happening. Journalists and photographers covered the conflict, and wired home their impressions and the photographs and live video feeds that defined the war in many ways. What follows are a number of these items, which had great effect on how people felt about the war.

Vo Nyugen Giap (l) and Ho Chi Minh (r), who fought the Japanese, the French and the Americans - and won

Vietnamese victory at Dien Bien Phu, 1954

Buddhist monk immolates himself to protest Diem's alignment with the West, 1963

Kennedy and Diem: JFK wanted Diem removed from power and exiled. The CIA took that to mean assassination. 1963

Exhausted and wounded American troops, Vietnam

Tet Offensive 1968: South Viet officer executes suspected Viet Cong guerrilla. A US military victory, the Tet Offensive was in many ways a North Vietnamese propaganda and moral victory

Nick Ut's famous "Napalm Girl" photo. The severely burned young girl survived a US napalm attack on her village. This photo caused widespread outrage in the United States and the world

Pres. Johnson listens to his son in laws' account of fighting in Vietnam

1st Photos of Viet Mass Slaying

WEATHER
Warm Showers and colder today.
High in the upper 50s
Details on Page 4-C

THE PLAIN DEALER

FINAL
Stocks & Races
Dow-Jones off 8.21

OHIO'S LARGEST NEWSPAPER

128TH YEAR—NO. 324 ★ ★ ★ ★ ★
CLEVELAND, THURSDAY, NOVEMBER 20, 1969
96 PAGES   10 CENTS

Exclusive

This photograph will shock Americans as it shocked the editors and the staff of The Plain Dealer. It was taken by a young Cleveland area man while serving as a photographer with the U.S. Army in South Vietnam.

It was taken during the attack by American soldiers on the South Vietnamese village My Lai, an attack which has made world headlines in recent days with disclosures of mass killings allegedly at the hands of American soldiers.

This photograph and others on two special pages are the first to be published anywhere of the killings.

This particular picture shows a clump of bodies of South Vietnamese civilians which includes women and children. Why they were killed raises one of the most momentous questions of the war in Vietnam.

Cameraman Saw GIs Slay 100 Villagers

By JOSEPH ESZTERHAS
(c) 1969, The Plain Dealer

A clump of bodies on a road in South Vietnam.

My Lai Massacre, 1968. News of US troops killing of Vietnamese villagers came out a year later, reigniting opposition against the war, below.

1973: US POW Robert Stirm returns to his family. 1973 marked the end of US military involvement in South Vietnam

April 1975: As North Vietnamese take over the South, American Embassy staff and refugees attempt to get aboard the last US helicopter out of Vietnam

Chapter 2: The Green Beret

Many of the headlines describing the combat action and missions of the 21st century American military are about the "Special Forces". Today's "Special Forces" consist of groups such as the Air Forces' Special Operations Command, which includes units specially trained for search and rescue of downed pilots, reconnaissance of future targets, etc. The Marines Special Operations Regiment, or "Raiders", named after the first Marine special force in WWII, and of course the Navy SEAL's and Delta Force, which is recruited from men from all Special Forces units, and the Army's 75th Ranger Regiment – the various Ranger units themselves sometimes considered special operations units, or carrying out Special Forces type missions.

However, before these units took hold of the American imagination, there were the "Green Berets". The name "Green Berets" can be a bit confusing. The name is a colloquial one for the US Army's Special Forces Groups, which contain personnel that have formerly been in other specialized or elite units, such as the airborne or Rangers or both. During the Vietnam conflict, the name "Green Beret" was enough for most people to understand that the soldier or soldiers in question were among the best of the best the United States armed forces had to offer.

During WWII, the efficacy of small specialized, highly trained units made up from men culled from other formations was made clear. With the formation of the Commando's of the United Kingdom, and men from other Allied nations in exile, such as Holland, Norway, Belgium, etc, and continuing with the development of the now famous Special Air Service, or "SAS" and their successful exploits, the United States also realized the immense value of having special units at their disposal. Some of the first units, and the ancestors of today's Special Forces units of all American military branches were Colonel William O. Darby's "Rangers", the joint US-Canadian 1st Special

Service Force, the Marine Recon units under Carlson and Edson in the South Pacific and the Naval Underwater Demolition (UDT) and Naval Construction and Demolitions Units (NCDU) teams which operated in both Europe and the Pacific.

These units, whether in Britain or the United States, had enemies among the more traditional military establishment. Many believed that the irregular nature and both perceived and real lack of discipline on the part of many of these special forces units were contrary to what many believed were the image and role of the traditional military. The advent of nuclear weapons, missiles, and long range nuclear bombers also led some to believe that ground soldiers of all types were soon to be redundant. Many of these units were disbanded or reduced in size after WWII

Still, there were those that did see the need for specialized units and in the period after WWII to the early 1950, the need for a small cadre of specialized troops was kept alive. The first Special Forces units were formed in 1952, and were active in many parts of the world before the large-scale involvement of the United States' in Vietnam. The units distinctive Green Beret was initially frowned upon, and was even banned for a time, but President John Kennedy, a veteran himself, understood the need for a unifying badge of honor for this elite unit. It was in Vietnam that the legend of the "The Green Berets" began.

The Green Berets entered mainstream American consciousness with the publication of Robin Moore's 1966 bestseller, "The Green Berets". Before the publication of Moore's book, many Americans knew of their nations increased involvement in Southeast Asia, but did not know exactly who was involved. News stories and the statements of the Kennedy then Johnson administrations mentioned "advisers" to the South Vietnamese military, but outside of a very few, most people in the United States did not know who these "advisers" were. With the publication of Moore's book, they did.

Moore was a friend and Harvard classmate of Robert Kennedy, the president's brother and Attorney General of the United States. With friends in very high places, Moore was given access to the very private world of the Special Forces as they existed in the early 1960's. Additionally, the general in charge of Special Forces insisted that if Moore was to report on the training of the unit, he would undergo the same training that Special Forces candidates did. He completed the rigorous course, and was allowed to accompany, as a civilian, Special Forces units to Southeast Asia where they were training the South Vietnamese Army – both regular and irregular units.

Special Forces units had been working since the late 1950's on strategies and tactics to defeat the communist guerrillas sponsored by North Vietnam. These guerrillas were known until 1959 as the "Viet Minh" (short for "League for the Independence of Vietnam"), and known worldwide after 1960 by the contraction "Viet Cong", which has many translations, all of which lead back to one basic meaning: "Vietnamese Communist".

Moore's book was so popular that it spawned a movie of the same name, starring John Wayne. This happened to be one of Wayne's worst. In that terribly clichéd film however, were events based on the battle in which the first American in Vietnam won the Medal of Honor.

Included in Moore's book were some of the tactics and methods the counter-insurgent Green Beret advisers utilized in Vietnam. Some of the book was edited by Army censors and Moore was forced to publish the book as fiction. Nonetheless, it was a phenomenal best-seller.

Part of the reason for the book's success was growing public interest in America's role in Vietnam and the Special Forces in general. Much of this interest was spurred on by the awarding of the Medal of Honor to Captain (later Colonel) Roger Donlon in late 1964. Though it could not be known at the time, Donlon's citation was the first of two hundred forty six Medals' of Honor won in Vietnam. His award was also the first given to a member of the Special Forces.

Roger Donlon was born in Saugerties, New York in 1934. Saugerties lies north of New York City and is not far from the site of the Woodstock Concert of 1969. In many ways, Roger Donlon was the typical "All-American" boy of the time: blond, blue eyed, long time Boy Scout, outstanding high school athlete, and president of his high school junior class. Roger was one of ten children whose father was a WWI combat veteran, and all of his brothers served in the armed forces, one of them being wounded in action.

Roger graduated in 1952 and enrolled in Air Force ROTC before transferring to the Military Academy at West Point. After two years at the Academy, family issues brought him home to New York. In 1959, he was commissioned a second lieutenant after completing Officer's Candidate School. He then served as a general's aide, but after two and a half years grew tired of office duty.

One of the common traits in men, and now women, in the elite units of the armed forces is that they both want to serve with the best, and see what they are truly made of. Roger Donlon was that type of person. He underwent Special Forces training in 1963, and was deployed to Vietnam in May of 1964.

In addition to training South Vietnamese forces, the Green Berets were to keep an eye on the movements and development of both the underground resistance movement in the South (the Viet Cong), and the

Donlon in Vietnam, 1964

role of the North Vietnamese Army (NVA) throughout the country. Observation posts were established as bases of operations for intelligence gathering and reconnaissance throughout the country, and especially in the more remote areas bordering Vietnam's neighbors of Laos and Cambodia. The camp commanded by Captain Donlon was located by the Laotian border of both South and North Vietnam in the district of the same name. It s located about thirty miles west of the large city of Da Nang, which would later become a familiar name to Americans.

Manning the outpost were three hundred sixty South Vietnamese troops being supervised and trained by twelve US Special Forces personnel, and one Australian artillery officer and adviser, Warrant Officer Kevin Conway, who was killed in the Nam Dong battle.

Donlon and the twelve men of his team set up the Nam Dong camp in May 1964. Almost immediately, the Americans and the Vietnamese stationed there began to conduct patrols in the area and to question the people of the area about Viet Cong or North Vietnamese activity in the area.

Among the three hundred sixty Vietnamese troops with Donlon and his Green Berets at Nam Dong were about sixty men from the Nung ethnic group. Vietnam is made up of fifty distinct ethnic groups. The majority are the Viet, which in 2014 make up over eighty-five percent of the population of approximately ninety-five million people. Fifteen million belong to various minorities, many of whom live in the mountainous border areas of the nation. In the 1950's and '60s many of these people were against centralized rule either from Saigon (the capital of South Vietnam), or Hanoi (the capital of North Vietnam). Among these mountain tribes were also large numbers of people who were strongly anti-communist.

Though the month and a half that Donlon and his team had been in Vietnam had been relatively quiet, the young captain from New York and his American comrades had a strange sense that that was about to change. In an area where they had been told that North Vietnamese regulars had passed through and communist recruitment been recently active, nothing was happening. That in itself was strange.

On July 4, there was an incident within the camp that put Donlon and the other Americans on alert and on edge. For some time, they had suspected that a number of the Vietnamese within the camp were actually communist sympathizers, and there was a brief shootout between one of these men and the other men of the unit. The man was killed, but Donlon and the other Americans suspicions had been confirmed. There was no practical way, however, of rooting out suspected insurgents without completely disrupting the camp and eliminating its usefulness. In all likelihood, the violent outburst was ordered by the communists in order to put the camp on edge and deliberately sow suspicion within it.

At 230am on the morning of 6 July 1964, the battle of Nam Dong began. Approximately nine hundred Viet Cong guerrillas besieged the base for five hours during the darkness and early morning light. Though many of the defenders, American, Vietnamese, and Australian, fought valiantly, it was the leadership and actions of Roger Donlon that most likely made the difference between victory and defeat.

Camp A-726 at Nam Dong, 1964

The Viet Cong opened the battle with an intense mortar barrage, but the training of the Green Berets kicked in immediately and within moments, the Americans and Vietnamese and Australian Warrant Officer Conway began a counter-barrage. Throughout the area, the "VC" (just one of the many nicknames by which the Viet Cong would become known) used loudspeakers to encourage their Vietnamese countrymen to turn on the American advisers or promised safe conduct for the troops within the camp if they turned the Americans over. This happened a number of times during the battle, and at times, Donlon the other Americans and loyal Vietnamese had to encourage their own men to fight.

At various times throughout the battle, Donlon's fears about VC infiltrators came true. These men were instructed to remove their South

Vietnamese or American issued uniforms to reveal a brightly colored loin that would identify them to the Viet Cong assaulting the camp. They were also instructed to cut the throat or shoot those sharing foxholes with them. These men caused a number of casualties among the Vietnamese fighting with the Americans and kept everyone on edge. Some of these men were killed during the battle, others fled into the forest after it was over.

As the battle grew in intensity, Donlon and the other Americans along with the Vietnamese soldiers they were sure of redeployed into an inner redoubt of trenches and bunkers, where they swore they would not be taken alive. Later Donlon said that he and the other Americans estimated the number of VC sympathizers at twenty men within the camp. Later it became evident as these communist agents either turned on nearby comrades or joined the assaulting VC that the number was nearer one hundred. The fact that the Americans and their loyal Vietnamese comrades had to fight the enemy without and *within* their camp makes their victory even more incredible.

All wars are political, but Vietnam was to be the most politicized war the United States ever fought. In Donlon's Medal of Honor citation and other public accounts, it makes no mention of the VC sympathizers. Why? To do so would be to admit to the American public that the cause of the VC was much more popular in the country than had been admitted and second, that attempts to screen sympathizers out of the South Vietnamese Army had failed.

Donlon seemed to be everywhere during the battle. When the VC barrage first started coming down on them, he organized counter-battery fire and helped to remove much needed ammunition from a building that had caught fire.

As the battle grew in intensity, Green Beret medic, Sergeant Terrance Terrin, informed Donlon that casualties were starting to mount and that the Americans had suffered their first death, Sergeant John Houston, the forces' radio operator, who wife had just sent word to Houston that she was expecting twins. Donlon paused to gather himself after hearing of the death of his comrade and friend and took it up the duties of his radioman as well.

In the next couple of years, as American involvement in Vietnam escalated, young men volunteering or being drafted into the US armed forces were relatively sure that their Vietnamese enemy would be a pushover. Like the men of WWII in the Pacific fighting the Japanese twenty years previous, many Americans had racial stereotypes that clouded their judgment about the fighting abilities of their enemy. Most Americans could not even find Vietnam on a map in 1964-65, and many did not know that the Vietnamese had been at war in some form or other for nearly a century. Though many of the Viet Cong and North Vietnamese Army were poor villagers with little or no education, they were led by battle-hardened veterans. Many had been part of the defeat of the French ten years before.

The VC knew what they were doing, and mounted a coordinated and heavy assault on the base at Nam Dong. Amid falling mortar shells, grenades flung from close range and heavy gunfire, Donlon organized the resistance of the camp.

After helping move the ammunition from the burning building, Donlon noticed that VC sappers (demolition men) were heading for the camps heavily reinforced main gate in order to destroy it and allow greater access to the assaulting force. As he ran to a position overlooking the enemy troops, he was targeted by enemy gunners and grenades, all of which missed their target. Donlon then dropped to one knee and took aim at the VC approaching the gate. "Click." No ammunition. During the mayhem of the battle, he had spent all of the little ammunition he had been carrying. Remaining in his position under fire, Donlon yelled to comrades in a nearby 60mm mortar pit nearby to throw him a magazine for his rifle. When he stooped to pick it up, it was still wrapped in the cardboard wrapper it came in. The captain quickly flicked three rounds from the top of the magazine, firing each round and loading the next, killing all three enemy sappers.

As Donlon dispatched the enemy sappers at the main gate, the men of the nearby mortar pit took a hit. Making his way to their position, Captain Donlon was seriously wounded in the abdomen. When he jumped into the pit, he saw that the men within it were also wounded, and ordered their evacuation to a safer location. As those men helped each other to the rear, Donlon provided covering fire. The captain then noticed that his staff sergeant was too seriously wounded to evacuate the mortar pit on his own, so Donlon dragged him out of the pit himself. As two other men came to the sergeant's aid and moved him to safety, an enemy mortar shell exploded nearby, tearing a gash in Donlon's left shoulder.

Determined to carry on despite his wounds, Donlon got back into the mortar pit, shouldered the 60mm mortar, and brought it to another position, where he discovered three other wounded men. Ignoring both his own wounds and the gunfire around him, Donlon applied first aid to these three men, encouraged them to continue fighting and set up the 60mm in their position while he returned to the abandoned position to retrieve the weapons' ammo.

On his return trip, he first stopped at another empty position and retrieved a heavy shoulder fired 57mm recoilless rifle. Dragging this along with him, he returned to the first mortar pit, retrieved ammunition for both the 60mm and the recoilless rifle. As he carried/dragged his load back to his men, Donlon was wounded a third time, this time catching grenade fragments in his leg and literally being blown out of his boots. Sometime during the evening he also sustained a concussion. None of this stopped Roger Donlon.

In this condition, Captain Donlon crawled nearly two hundred yards to another mortar position on the other side of the camp, this time an heavy 81mm unit, where he coordinated to repel a renewed enemy effort to break through on the east side of the outpost. He then returned the two hundred yards to the first 60mm mortar pit and assisted two wounded Vietnamese there in setting up and firing the weapon. Once confident in their ability to defend themselves, Donlon moved to other positions around the perimeter of the camp, firing on enemy troops and throwing hand grenades despite his wounds.

While Captain Donlon was performing his heroics, two other men were doing the same – at the cost of their lives. Australian Kevin Conway and Green Beret Master Sergeant Gabriel Alamo manned a mortar pit together when the enemy attack began. Sergeant Alamo was killed early in the fighting, and Conway fired his mortar alone, slowing the advance of the approaching enemy, until he was forced to fire his weapon at such a trajectory that the shells would likely fall back onto his position. This is exactly what he did, stalling the enemy advance long enough for his comrades to fill the gaps in the line but at the cost of his own life. Conway, Alamo, and Houston were the three Westerners killed at Nam Dong, along with nearly one hundred of their brave Vietnamese allies.

All of this action occurred at night. The only real illumination was from shell and gunfire, explosions and flares. As day started to break over the camp, the enemy assault began to wind down, but it was not over yet. Donlon used the growing light to assess the damage of the previous few hours and strengthened his defenses. As he did, an enemy mortar exploded nearby, spraying him with shell fragments in the face and body. Despite this, he refused to be evacuated to the camp's medical bay until he was sure its defenses were secure.

Not only did Donlon's actions inspire those in America when they were publicized, but the South Vietnamese soldiers that had fought under his command were astonished by Donlon's actions and bravery. They and many other non-communist South Vietnamese, who had questioned the American's commitment to their defense, no longer did so.

At dawn turned into daylight, the enemy faded back into the forest, leaving nearly sixty of their dead behind with many more wounded. The Americans and Vietnamese at Nam Dong had sustained more casualties, but had driven off a numerically superior enemy.

On Thanksgiving Day 1964, while at home on leave and recovering from his many wounds, Captain Donlon received word that he would be awarded the Medal of Honor, which was given him by President Johnson at the White House on December 5th.

The Johnson Administration, in its announcement of Donlon's Medal of Honor, made the following statement:

"*This is the first Medal of Honor awarded to an individual who distinguished himself while serving with a friendly force engaged in an armed conflict in which the United States is not a belligerent party.*"

Unfortunately, this was just the beginning of the political double-speak which marred the actions of men like Captain Donlon during the Vietnam War from start to finish.

Chapter 3: Medic!

Though they may not be the best-known war heroes, many combat veterans will tell you that the bravest men they have ever seen on the battlefield were the combat medic or, as they are known in the Navy and Marines, "Corpsmen".

Though the armed forces of the United States have always included doctors and other medical personnel, it was not until the 20th century that medical personnel had a real and sizable role on the battlefield.

From the Revolutionary War to the beginning of the Civil War, doctors and/or surgeons served with or volunteered for duty, but were for the most part located miles away from the battlefield. Wounded men on the battlefield tended each other with homemade bandages and sometimes applied homemade, down on the farm type cures. Needless to say, the fatality rate for those wounded beyond the superficial was high. Of course, the doctors, nurses, and medics of both the Revolutionary Era and modern times had/have to deal with much more than wounds sustained in combat. Actually, until the 20th century, more men died from disease than as a result of combat with the enemy.

In the first year and a half of the American Civil War, medical and hygienic conditions were horrendous. Water supplies were frequently tainted by dead bodies buried to close to a water source, and bodies frequently lay about on the battlefield and near medical tents for days, attracting disease carrying flies and vermin.

If this was not enough to kill you, being operated on just might. At the start of the Civil War, germ theory (the idea that microscopic organisms caused and contributed to disease) was just that – a theory. Though some noted scientists, doctors, nurses and learned laymen subscribed to the idea, many did not and conditions reflected it. Surgeons would be covered in the blood of the last patient, without gloves, and dive right into the next operation. Sterilized instruments were virtually non-existent. Mountains of amputated limbs stood outside medical tents, further spreading disease. Those who had limbs amputated were just as likely to die as those who did not.

The conditions in Union hospitals came to the attention of the public and officials, and change, including better sanitary practices, organization and uniform practices, came rapidly. By the end of the war, the survival rate for wounded men who reached the hospital almost doubled. One of the leading advocates of this change was Major Jonathan Letterman. This is the surgeon who was the namesake of the famous Letterman Army Hospital in the Presidio in San Francisco, and who convinced his superiors to create a separate medical branch of the United States Army, which was responsible for hospitals, ambulances and much more.

Of course, there were some improvements in medical science within and outside of the military in the years between the Civil War and WWI, but they came slowly. This was evidenced by the horrendous death rate from yellow fever and other diseases during the Spanish-American War in 1898 and the Philippine Uprising afterwards.

The wars of the early 20th century, WWI and WWII saw great leaps forward in combat medicine. It was in WWII that more effective treatment of combat wounded took a revolutionary step. Combat troops would be joined by combat medics trained in first aid and basic surgical techniques. First aid stations were placed nearer the front than previously, designed to operate on those in immediate need of stabilization/life saving surgery, and then they and other wounded men would be transferred further to the rear at more permanent and well-equipped installations.

The integration of the helicopter into medical service also began to have an effect, starting in the Korean War (1950-1953). This was famously depicted in the book, movie, and TV series M*A*S*H (Mobile Army Surgical Hospital). Capable of reaching places that wheeled or tracked vehicles could not get to, or could only get to slowly, helicopters could pick up wounded soldiers and have them on the way to a hospital in relatively short order.

As medical knowledge expanded, so did the training of combat medics and Corpsmen. An Army report written after the Vietnam War noted that a man wounded on the field of battle in Vietnam had a better chance of survival that a severe accident victim on the freeways of California.

There are a couple of myths about the combat medic/Corpsman. We will refer to Corpsmen as medics from here on out for simplicity. Firstly, that they were all unarmed. This is not true. Some indeed carried no weapons, but some did, especially in the jungle fighting that took place on the islands of WWII when men taken by the Japanese had a very short life expectancy.

In Europe, medics carrying weapons were rarer, for a number of reasons. German medics rarely if ever carried weapons, and they expected the medics of the Western Allies to do the same. Harsh treatment was sometimes doled out to medics captured with arms. On the Eastern Front of WWII all rules of warfare were off. Armed or not, Russian and German medics were fair game and open targets, captive or otherwise.

Some medics in WWII and beyond did not carry weapons because it allowed them to carry additional kit that might be needed to save someone's life. Others, like Thomas Bennett, who you will read about below, were conscientious objectors and refused to carry a weapon or take a human life. Many medics in the Vietnam War carried a .45 caliber pistol and many carried M-16's. Being taken prisoner by the Viet Cong or NVA was not a pleasant experience.

Medics in Vietnam generally enjoyed certain latitude when it came to the medical equipment they carried. Some found one piece of equipment particularly useful (for its original or an improvised use), while others could make due without it. Broadly speaking, the combat medic of Vietnam in the 1960's carried inside his one or two aid bags and on his person:

SURGICAL SHEET

JACKSON SIZE 3 TRACHEOTOMY CANNULA

1 MINOR SURGERY FIELD INSTRUMENT

2 ARMY TOURNIQUETS

1 BOX OF COTTON SWABS ON A WOODEN STICK

1 TIN OF REXALL SURGICAL POWDER

2 BOTTLES OF WATER PURIFICATION TABLETS

1 TIN OF SUNBURN PREVENTITIV8 GAUZE PETROLATUM DRESSINGS

2 - 11 3/4 INCH SQUARE DYED FIRST AID FIELD DRESSINGS

1 FIELD EYE DRESSING KIT

VITAMIN E CREAM

4 TONGUE DEPRESSORS

1- 4 INCH COTTON ELASTIC BANDAGE

2- 3 INCH COTTON ELASTIC BANDAGES

1- 3 INCH X 10 YARDS CAMOUFLAGED GAUZE BANDAGE

3 TRIANGULAR BANDAGES

4 ROUND CONTAINERS OF 1 INCH X 6 YARDS GAUZE ROLLER

1- 24 X 72 INCH GAUZE COMPRESS

1 INDIVIDUAL FIRST AID FIELD DRESSING

1- 3 INCH X 6 YARDS CAMOUFLAGED GAUZE BANDAGE

3 BOXES OF FIELD BAND-AIDS

1 BOX OF 10 AMMONIA INHALANTS

1 TUBE OF TANNIC ACID JELLY BURN COMPOUND

1 FIELD DRESSING IN A BROWN WRAPPER

1 TUBE OF PETROLINE BACITRACIN OINTMENT

1 TUBE OF OPTHALMIC OINTMENT FOR EYE INFECTIONS

1 PACKAGE OF 4 - 2X2 CAMOUFLAGED COMPRESS AND BANDAGE 1 TIN OF REXALL QUIK-BANDS BAND-AIDS

2 BOXES OF 1 INCH X 6 YARDS GAUZE

1 BOX OF 3 INCH X 10 YARDS GAUZE ROLLER PLAIN

1 BOX OF 10 MERTHIOLATE SWABS

2-4 CANTEENS WATER

And the medic or one of his comrades likely carried one, or more, last piece of equipment – the "body bag."

One of the most famous soldiers in the history of the United States was Sergeant Alvin York. Deeply religious, he registered for the draft as required by the law of the time, but expressed his desire to serve in a non-combat capacity, as his religious beliefs were strongly pacifist in outlook. After deep meditation, York volunteered for combat duty. He could not refuse danger while his friends and comrades were risking and losing their lives. Sergeant York ended the war as American's greatest hero.

There were essentially two types of conscientious objector before Vietnam: those who would join the armed forces and serve in a non-combat capacity, and those who completely refused service on religious grounds. The Vietnam conflict gave rise to another type of conscientious objector – one who refused to serve for political reasons. Thirty-two years after the end of the American involvement in the conflict, questions about the draft, conscientious objection and much more about the conflict are still deeply felt on all sides. This small introductory e-book is not the place for a political debate. The essential fact, for this part of our book, is that there were for various reasons conscientious objectors during the Vietnam War. One of them was Corporal Thomas W. Bennett of West Virginia, who is one of two conscientious objectors (the other, Medic Desmond Doss, served in WWII) to have won the Medal of Honor for service to their country and comrades.

Bennett was from the small West Virginia city of Morgantown on the Monongahela River in 1947. Thomas was raised Southern Baptist and was a deeply religious young man. Many tens of thousands of Southern Baptists have served in the US Armed Forces as there is nothing in church doctrine that calls for pacifism during armed conflict. However, the Sixties called into question many beliefs and as he grew into a young man, Thomas Bennett formed opinions of his own. Going to the University of West Virginia also expanded his horizons and he sought out the views of other religious young adults and staff at the school. Over time, he came to oppose the taking of human life under virtually any circumstance, especially war. At the same time, childhood friends had entered the service, and one had lost his life. Tom did not want to shirk his duty while some had made the supreme sacrifice.

Thomas was not the best student on campus. He spent more time involved in athletics and other activities, he started the campus ecumenical council to bring members of all faiths together, when he should have been studying. As he was finishing his sophomore year he was placed on academic probation. College students, who made up a much smaller segment of the population than they do today, were given a deferment for the draft, as long as they successfully remained in school. This in itself was controversial, for though most of the soldiers that served in Vietnam were white, by a higher percentage of the black and Latino minorities served in the armed forces, as did poor whites. If he lost his college draft deferment, which he was sure he was going to, Bennett knew he would be drafted. He likely would have been able to enroll as a conscientious objector if drafted. However, should he choose to volunteer, the path would be that much easier. So in early 1968, Thomas enlisted and volunteered as a medic.

Thomas did not agree with the war for religious and political reasons – as many of the young people of America did in 1969, but he did not feel he had the right to avoid service when others of his generation were draftees and had no choice. He hoped that he would not see combat – after all, America had troops stationed worldwide. As it turns out, this was false hope: combat medics were needed in combat and the only combat America was engaged in during 1969 was in Vietnam. Tom was going to war, no doubt though he tried to convince himself and his family that that would not be the case.

Before he left for Vietnam, he took Christmas leave at home. Despite actually being proud of his uniform and for the most part displaying a brave face for his family, he broke down in front of his parents just before shipping out. "I can't do it. I can't go over there. Mother, I am too young to die." As many veterans will attest, anyone who says they were not afraid was either lying or mentally ill. Before he left, Bennett regained his confidence, and was as ready as he could be when he left for Southeast Asia on January 5th 1969.

New Years' Eve and New Years' Day 1969 were likely not days of celebration for Tom. While much of the rest of the world rang in the New Year with champagne and parties, Tom was getting ready to go to Vietnam. He would see combat, without doubt. Like most soldiers going into a war zone, he probably worried about his parents and family and if he would stand up to being under fire. In Tom's case, he had the additional worry that medics always carry before battle. Would he be able to function under fire, and would he make a mistake that might cost someone their life? Bennett did not have to wait long to find out.

On January 10, he was in Vietnam waiting to be assigned. Two days later, he found himself in the 4th Infantry Division, and on January 22, Tom found himself a member of Bravo Company, 1st Battalion, 14th Infantry Regiment, 4th Division deep in the Central Highlands of Vietnam, very far from Morgantown West Virginia.

Tom learned that despite having been in the area for the last seven months, Bravo Company had had no serious casualties and no losses. Its commanding officer, Captain Carrett Cowsert, was respected by his men and led them well. Enemy activity in the area of B Company and the 14th Regiment in general was minimal.

Unfortunately for Thomas Bennett that was about to change. Just after Tom arrived, NVA activity had been noticed in the area of a nearby hill called Chu Pa, and Bravo was ordered to climb the peak and surrounding areas and investigate. Nothing would get Tom in combat shape faster than carrying all of his equipment up a 5,000-foot mountain covered in jungle and ravines in the Vietnamese summer. After a week of climbing through the jungle in the intense humidity and heat, Bravo Company had found nothing. Back down the other side they went.

As they set up camp one night, Bennett used the tape recorder he had brought with him to record a message to his parents. They could not know it, but it was the last time they would hear his voice.

"...When you start adding up figures and taking percentages and stuff, over here there are very few places that I can be safer than with the U.S. Army...I feel that they can't hurt me in any way. I have had and am having such a rich, full, good exciting life that, well, nobody can take that away *from me. There's very little chance that anything's gonna happen. And if it does, so what? I've had my twenty-one good years..."*

After four days of investigating the other side of the mountain, Bravo Company was still moving downhill when on Bravo's left, its sister company, Delta (or "D") was caught in a North Vietnamese ambush. Tom's platoon was ordered to maneuver around the enemy and catch them in the rear, but before the men had gone a hundred yards, they too were ambushed.

The three men at the head of the platoon went down in the first burst of enemy fire. The rest of the men hit the deck – but not Thomas Bennett. He did not have to worry about what he would do in combat any longer. He moved low under fire to the wounded men and applied the first aid that probably kept each of the men alive.

Bennett was not a big man. He was only five and a half feet tall and slight, but he found the strength to carry each of the wounded men to relative safety. All of this was done while a firefight was raging around him.

After caring for the first three men, Tom returned to the center of the fighting, caring for wounded men. In the seven months before Tom's arrival, Bravo Company had suffered no deaths in combat. In short, minutes on February 9 1969, five men lost their lives and six suffered serious wounds. At least two of these men were pulled from open ground by Tom Bennett in plain view of the enemy.

Before the day ended, the enemy retreated into the jungle and Medevac helicopters flew in to take the most seriously wounded to the nearest Army hospital. Other wounded men remained in Tom's care. No one in his platoon really slept that night, but they stayed in their freshly dug foxholes in case the enemy returned during the night – all except the platoon medic who stayed awake all night caring for the men, hopping from hole to hole.

During the night, Platoon Sergeant James McBee, who was later awarded the Distinguished Service Cross for his actions that day, approached Captain Cowsert and recommended to his commander that Bennett be nominated for the Silver Star. Both the sergeant and the men of the platoon felt he deserved it. McBee told Cowsert that he had actually had to chew out the medic for taking too many risks, but Bennett had told the sergeant that it was God's will that he take care of the men and that if he (Bennett) died, that too was the will of God. Turned out that Thomas Bennett was not as afraid as he feared he might be.

The next day, Bravo Company began to move further down the steep jungle covered slope. A number of times they saw NVA soldiers in the distance pacing them. Each time the Americans made a move to fire or pursue, the NVA sprinted into the jungle, out of range. They were not burdened with the equipment of the Americans and kept up a game of cat and mouse all day. Though the Americans were the more heavily armed cat, the mice were the ones making the rules. In the late afternoon of February 10, the NVA once again hit Bravo Company hard.

In addition to the same heavy small arms fire they took the day before, Bravo was now taking rocket fire and more American dropped to the ground wounded. Periodically throughout the battle, the men stopped and stared in wonder as Tom Bennett ran out into the open to treat the wounds of his comrades. Machine gun, sniper, and rocket fire blazed all around, but Bennett remained both undaunted and unhurt. As the sun went down, the fighting ceased. For the second night in a row, the medic went without sleep, caring for his buddies in the darkness.

The next morning, the NVA let the Americans know they were still around – snipers hidden in the jungle took pot shots at the GI's in the early morning hours. Several more men were hit, some seriously, some superficially. Each time, Tom Bennett was there to help them.

As Bennett was gathering in strength in a foxhole with Sergeant McBee, someone yelled out in pain. A new man, whose name wasn't even known to most of the men in the platoon, much less the company, had been struck by a sniper's bullet. After crying out, he lay inert about thirty feet from Bennett and McBee's hole. As Bennett began to climb over the lip of the hole to get to the wounded man, Sergeant McBee grabbed him and said, "Don't go out there! He's gone." Tom had to see for himself. As he climbed out of his hole, NVA troops hidden in the bush opened up with their AK-47's. Tom Bennett was hit multiple times. By the time he slumped backwards into the foxhole, he was dead.

Tom's parents were asked to come to the White House on April 7, 1970 to receive the nation's highest honor from President Nixon. Tom's mother did not want to go. She too was against the war, and had she been a draft age male, would also have been a conscientious objector. Tom's step-dad was also against the war, but believed that the men Tom had saved and served with wanted him to be recognized and that to refuse the honor would be an insult to Tom's comrades in arms.

The fresh-faced Thomas Bennett was but one of the medics who were awarded the Medal of Honor during the Vietnam War. About a year earlier,

the Medal was bestowed on Private Clarence Sasser by President Nixon. Unlike Tom Bennett, Sasser was present for the ceremony, but on the day of the action for which he won the award, Clarence's presence anywhere in the future was in doubt.

Although they never met, Clarence and Tom Bennett's histories' had some things in common. Both left college and joined the army. Both were combat medics and both served only a relatively short time in Vietnam before performing the act for which they won the Medal of Honor. One thing they did not have in common was race. Tom was white and Clarence is black, but they also shared a love for, and a sense of responsibility to their comrades. That love and sense of duty cost Tom his life. It almost did the same for Clarence.

Clarence was born in 1947 in the small town of Chenango Texas, south of Houston and west of Galveston. Like many African-American families in the area, his farming family had a tough time making ends meet, but hard work kept the family afloat. He did well enough in high school to attend the University of Houston, where he majored in chemistry.

Clarence did not share Tom Bennett's ideas about war, nor Roger Donlon's. Like many young Americans at the time, Clarence was not keen in going to war in a country very few Americans really knew about. Unlike many other African-Americans who enlisted or were drafted into the armed forces at the time, Clarence, with his college career ahead of him and his aptitude, had a chance of staying out of the war altogether.

Unfortunately, Clarence needed to pay his own way through school, and though he had a part time job to help him while a full-time student, he could not make ends meet with the amount of time he was working. The increased work hours he took on meant that he had to go from a full-time student with a draft deferment to a part-time student with no draft deferment. He did not fully realize this until...the draft notice arrived. Clarence was drafted into the United States Army in 1967.

Clarence had attended college and majored in chemistry. The army actually got it right and judging by his intelligence tests and background, they sent him for training as a medic, which he picked up with relative ease.

After completing his training and shipping off to Vietnam, Clarence found himself with the Headquarters Company and then A Company of 3rd Battalion, 60th Infantry Regiment, 9th Infantry Division as a private. He had been in country for about a month and a half when his unit was attached to a helicopter-borne air assault reconnaissance mission on January 10, 1968.

Vietnam is a geographically diverse country. It is a long coastal strip which meets tropical jungle a few miles inland, primarily in the south. Running down much of the center of the country are the Central Highlands where Thomas Bennett was to die in action in 1969. These are heavily forested, with both dense jungle canopy and less dense deciduous forest. Much of the northern portion of the country is flat plains, at least near the coast. The very southern part of Vietnam consists of the delta area of the Mekong River, and this is where Clarence Sasser and his unit were deployed.

In movies and TV shows about Vietnam, the landscape is almost always the same: rice paddies surrounded by tree-lines and then jungle. Much of the Mekong Delta is swamp and tidal flats. It is extremely hot and humid almost all year long. Mosquitoes in swarms and snakes of all kinds infest the area, as do leeches in the water. Minefields in paddies were difficult to detect and the large open areas made finding cover difficult if not impossible should one be caught out in the open.

The Mekong Delta was a hotbed of Viet Cong activity and reports of sizable enemy movement brought orders for the heli-borne reconnaissance mission that Clarence found himself on.

As the half dozen or so Huey helicopters flew over the area where heavy VC activity had been reported, they were met by extremely heavy fire from the ground. Soldiers shot at the low-flying American machines with AK-47's, multiple heavy machine gun emplacements and rocket launchers.

Clarence was flying in the third or fourth helicopter and watched as one of the other helicopters crashed into the rice paddy after taking heavy enemy fire. Clarence's chopper and the others flew low and landed nearby to both rescue any survivors of the crash and engage the enemy.

The mission did not start well in general, and did not begin well for Clarence individually either. As he jumped down from the Huey, he was shot in the leg. Fortunately, it was only a grazing wound, but it was enough to make Clarence's movements more difficult than they would have been.

It is difficult if not impossible for anyone who has not been through the experience to know what is was like for the men of Clarence's unit, and the others who landed in the open, under fire in the rice paddies of Vietnam. Flat, water-filled farm fields that were more like swamps – and virtually no cover, either as protection from enemy fire or from the enemies' view. Clarence's unit had kicked over a hornet's nest, and the amount of fire coming from three sides was astounding. To make matters worse, the VC were working on making that four sides.

Within just a couple of minutes, over thirty men of Clarence's unit were cut down. This is where Clarence Sasser sprung into action. He ran through the water and mud of the rice paddy to reach the men closest to the enemy who had been struck down. Many were hit badly, most were screaming and some were crying for their mothers. Clarence did his best to patch up the men lying about the paddy, all the while occasionally having to expose himself to enemy fire as he knelt or reached for something in his medical kit.

Doing his best to stabilize as many of the wounded men as he could, Sasser shouldered one badly wounded man and moved him out of the line of fire of the enemy. Shortly thereafter, Clarence sustained his second wound.

A mortar shell went off nearby, filling the air with buzzing, hot fragments. His back to the explosion, Clarence caught dozens of small pieces of the burning metal in his left shoulder and upper back. As Sasser moved he could feel the razor sharp fragments cutting into the skin and muscles of his back, but he refused treatment. He then ran as best he could to the wounded men he had previously treated, miraculously making it through both machine gun rocket fire from recoilless rifles and rocket propelled grenades (RPG's).

For the next five hours, the men of A Company were literally pinned to the ground. Later, Clarence said that to raise ones' arm up into the air would have gotten in shot off in seconds – the fire was so intense. So Clarence and his comrades lay in the water and muck, doing their best to fire back at the VC who had much better position than the Americans.

Clarence had been in country for fifty days and after the treatment he had given the first men who had been wounded upon landing, common sense kicked in and the adrenaline coursing through his veins reached a relatively steady level. That is, steady for someone who has been wounded twice, has the fate of other men directly and literally in his hands, and is under constant enemy fire with the threat of death or capture imminent.

During these five hours of hell, Clarence had to drag his body through the water and mud of the rice paddy for two reasons. First, raising himself up above the rice stalks was suicide. Second, even if he had wanted to get up (which he did not) and make his way more quickly to wounded men, he couldn't have. For by this time, in additional to the grazing wound he received on exiting the chopper and the shrapnel in his left shoulder, he had been wounded a further two times – once in each leg. They would not have supported him should he have wanted to stand. Clarence improvised – he used his arms to grab clumps of rice stalks and drag himself through the water and mud to get to his buddies. He did this despite being faint from blood loss, thirst and being under fire. He refused to listen to his sergeant and get care himself – for five long hours, while other men bled, screamed and some died. Many were saved by Sasser's actions that day.

If anything went right that day, it was that A Company was not overrun. This was prevented by the constant air cover provided by US warplanes stationed nearby, which flew in rotations for the five hours that A Company was under siege. Strafing runs with cannon, bombs and napalm rained down on the Viet Cong in their prepared positions. After five long hours, the VC ended their assault on A Company. Sasser and the men he cared for were evacuated to the nearest hospital, their ordeal finally over.

Clarence recovered relatively quickly from his wounds, and was nominated for the Medal of Honor shortly thereafter. When he returned to the United States after finishing his tour working in a hospital, he and his very proud mother were welcomed to the White House and given the Medal by President Nixon. Clarence retired a short time ago after finishing his career at the Bureau of Veterans Affairs, still helping his fellow veterans.

Chapter 4: The Delta and Its Hero

In 2004, the presidential election campaign in the United States again illustrated the strength that the Vietnam War and its memories had on the American psyche. The Vietnam War record of Democratic presidential candidate, Senator (Secretary of State in 2015) John Kerry of Massachusetts was attacked in a public campaign to throw a shadow over his time in the service. Kerry had been wounded multiple times in Vietnam and been awarded both the Bronze and Silver Stars.

The "Swift Boat Veterans for Truth" or SBVT, an organization of some veterans who had served in the same capacity as Kerry during the war, on riverine patrol aboard heavily armed and fast patrol boats, was organized by Texas Republican supporter and millionaire T. Boone Pickens and others. The men in SBVT were partly angry over Kerry's very public stance as an awarded combat veteran when he came home from Vietnam and believed him to be a bad choice for president.

At a time when the United States was again involved in war, Iraq and Afghanistan, Kerry felt the need to answer the allegations made by the SBVT. They claimed that his awards were pushed through channels without proper oversight, and that he did not really earn them in the first place.

Numerous Navy and government reports made clear that Kerry's awards had been properly earned and cleared. Veterans who had served *with* Kerry, some of them Republicans, publicly proclaimed his combat record. No matter – the constant and well-funded proclamations of the SBVT won out and were partially responsible for Kerry's losing the race. A new political term "swift boating" came into the American consciousness – a synonym for a public smear campaign. (For information regarding the

veracity of Kerry's war record, and the Navy report backing it up in 2004, see "John Kerry's Vietnam Crew-mates still fighting Swift Boating" in the Washington Post,
http://voices.washingtonpost.com/sleuth/2008/06/john_kerrys_vietnam_crew_mates.html

In the opinion of this author, who is a member of neither US political party, John Kerry is an average Secretary of State and I disagree with many of his opinions. At the same time, I believe he has served his country honorably for most of his life, even when criticizing its policies after his tour in Vietnam was over. Free Speech is part of what people fight for.

These opening paragraphs are meant to show the lasting impact of the Vietnam War, forty years after the last Americans were evacuated from the US Embassy in Saigon. It is also to introduce the reader to another overlooked aspect of the conflict, the riverine forces that patrolled the Mekong Delta, rivers, and bays of Vietnam during the war, of which the "swift boats" were a part.

The complete domination by the US Navy of the South China Sea that borders Vietnam to the east and the almost complete lack of any naval force whatsoever on the part of Vietnam, meant that Vietnam was mostly a land war. Though American Navy pilots, most famously, another presidential candidate, John McCain, flew countless missions over Vietnam and Southeast Asia, ships of the US Navy rarely engaged in any type of action.

The fighting that was to be done on the water took place on the rivers and their shores of South Vietnam. These were carried out by the Navy's "Riverine Forces" as they were designated in the 1960's and 70's.

If you read my "WW2 Sailor's Stories: Tales from Our Warriors at Sea", (http://www.amazon.com/World-War-Sailor-Stories-Warriors-ebook/dp/B00PRET5OG), you will read a chapter on the exploits of the

Navy's Patrol Torpedo Boats, or "PT Boats". Some of the most famous naval stories of WWII emerged from the adventures of the PT Boats and their crews, among them future President of the United States John F. Kennedy and John Bulkeley, subject of the famous John Wayne film, "They Were Expendable". The success of the PT crews and the utility of their vessels encouraged the Navy to form a similar force during the Vietnam War. The concept was not new. Coastal, or "littoral", craft had been part of US Naval and Marine strategy since the American Revolution, but it was the heavily armed PT Boats and their success in WWII which provided the impetus to the riverine program.

PBR (Patrol Boat, River) on patrol in Vietnam

One of the prime movers behind the concept of the program was a WWII hero, Captain Phil Hinkle Bucklew, considered by many to be one of the Founding Fathers of the Navy SEAL's. Bucklew, who had been awarded the Bronze Star, Silver Star, and twice the Navy Cross for his actions during the war, had started the conflict in Europe (taking part in the invasions of Sicily, Italy and Normandy) and ended it in Asia, working the coasts and rivers of China in an effort to aid the Chinese against their Japanese oppressors. Bucklew had then gone on the serve during the Korean Conflict of the early 1950's.

Bucklew was facing mandatory retirement when he got a sort of "reprieve" from President Kennedy in 1962. Kennedy, who was a major supporter of irregular operations, as we have seen from his support of the Green Berets, ordered the Navy to form a similar unit. Out of the experience of naval units in WWII and officers like Bucklew, the SEAL's were born. Bucklew was put in command of a number of Special Forces units, including two Underwater Demolition Teams ("UDT"), a waterborne support unit, and

SEAL Team One. (For more information about the evolution of Navy Special Warfare units, see my "WW2 Navy SEAL's: True Stories from the First Navy SEALs: The Amphibious Scout & Raiders." http://www.amazon.com/World-War-Navy-SEALs-Amphibious-ebook/dp/B00T256BNE/ref=sr_1_1?s=digital-text&ie=UTF8&qid=1427565850&sr=1-1&keywords=ryan+jenkins+WWII+SEALs)

As you have read, the United States became increasingly involved in Vietnam in the early 1960's. One of the first things that Bucklew and others that truly had their eyes open to the nature of the conflict and the enemy, realized was that much of the war would depend on counter-insurgency operations, not the set-piece battles that the United States had been fighting in WWII and Korea. There were many facets to the enemies' underground efforts during the war, but one of the most significant was their ability to get supplies from North Vietnam and China into the south.

The Viet Cong and North Vietnamese were not constrained by the same rules of engagement and politics that the United States was. To supply their forces in the south, the North Vietnamese were prepared to violate the borders of their neighbors, Laos and Cambodia, both of which had significant communist movements themselves. Additionally, the geography of Vietnam, with its jungles, mountains, dense forests, and long coastline and rivers, made supplying the insurgency a relatively easy proposition.

The VC supply effort was made easier by a number of factors. One was the inability or reluctance of the United States to cross the borders of Laos and Cambodia. Though most in Congress in the early 1960's supported the US effort to defeat communism in Vietnam, they were not willing to authorize or finance excursions into the neighboring countries. As the war ground on and became more unpopular across the nation and within the government, there was even less support for any border violations. This was made clear when Congress found out about Richard Nixon's secret authorization of land incursions and air raids in Cambodia in 1970.

Another factor aiding the VC effort was that like most insurgent/guerrilla operations, much of the VC effort was disguised as civilian trade and transportation. The United States, at least publicly, refused to acknowledge the amount of civilian support the VC had in South Vietnam. This was support that greatly aided the enemy.

At the beginning of 1964, Bucklew was requested to go to Vietnam and report on the enemy effort to supply troops within South Vietnam. What he found, after interviewing dozens of Americans and Vietnamese, was that the VC had an extensive supply route throughout the country, and much of it was water-borne. Bucklew saw with his own eyes the loading of arms and other supplies on native boats near the Cambodian border – an operation that took place in broad daylight.

Bucklew's conclusion was that a large-scale water-borne effort by the United States was needed if America was going to interdict and interrupt these supplies and effort. This effort would involve land-based forces such as the SEAL's and others, South Vietnamese infiltration and observation of VC units or trade routes and the cooperation of pro-US/South Vietnamese government civilians.

Unfortunately, for the forces of the United States and the fighting which came afterwards, the recommendations of Bucklew and others on this subject were almost completely disregarded until a number of years later. Though the force that developed along the lines that Bucklew had imagined did put a dent in the supplies getting to the VC in the South when they were developed, the Viet Cong and North Vietnamese stayed one-step ahead of the forces of the United States during the war. This showed itself in the full-scale offensive that the VC and NVA were able to launch all over South Vietnam during the Tet Offensive in 1968.

The difficulty of intercepting supplies is illustrated by the photo below, which was taken after the Vietnam conflict. The design of boats used for commerce on the rivers, bays, and streams of Vietnam has not changed in over a century of more.

Vietnamese sampans on an inland canal

The picture above was actually taken on a canal dug through the jungle leading from one river to another – another factor that made interdiction even harder. However, the rivers of South Vietnam, especially as they reach the coast, are wide, deep, and fast moving. At any one time during the day near Saigon, the rivers will almost be covered in boats and ships of various sizes. The Mekong River, which was one of the main supply routes for the North Vietnamese and the Viet Cong, is one of the world's largest and longest rivers. It was and is one of the main trade routes for the

nations of the region.

Though the picture above shows one of the busier water markets in southern Vietnam today, the Mekong River, along with others, such as the Bassac and Pearl, sometimes teem with boats in the more populated areas. There is no possible way to stop and search all of them, and attempting to do so would have alienated any Vietnamese that were still loyal to the South Vietnamese government and counted on American protection for their capitalist way of life on the river.

In the further reaches of the rivers, nearer to the borders of Cambodia, the waterway narrows and the traffic becomes a bit sparser. This however presents another problem, size. This is one of the reasons that the Swift boats, PBR's, and other variations were designed and put to use.

Another of the missions of the riverine forces was place American and South Vietnamese forces into the jungle, forest, and trade routes that might not be accessible in any other way. The boats, especially if traveling by night, also left less of a "footprint" than a sizable force moving overland, or large formations of helicopters flying over populated areas.

The PBR's and Swift boats transported SEAL's and other special forces units from the Navy, Marines and the Army deep into enemy controlled territory, carried out fire support missions when nearby, and brought supplies, medical attention and a method of evacuation/exfiltration. This

Swift Boat on the Mekong River

type of mission was made famous in the movie "Apocalypse Now" (1979). They were also supported and supplied by larger ships, usually converted tank landing ships from WWII

The Mekong Delta area covers more than forty thousand square miles of extraordinarily difficult terrain and waterways. Over the centuries, for reasons of nature, trade, secrecy, warfare, and privacy, an unknown number of waterways have been carved through the delta by erosion, rainfall, and mankind. To anyone not familiar with the landscape and climate, being in the Mekong Delta is almost like being on another planet. Men will adapt themselves to almost any conditions, but the men of the US armed forces, especially those from the city and those from the northern parts of the country, found themselves struggling to acclimatize themselves to the Mekong. Generally, the ones who did so more rapidly and successfully were from the southern coastal areas of the United States, where much of the terrain and climate bears at least some resemblance to the Delta area.

One such man was Petty Officer/Chief Boatswain's Mate James E. Williams of Darlington, South Carolina. Though located inland about seventy-miles from the Atlantic Coast, Darlington lies near the Pee Dee River and its many streams and territories. Though vastly different from the Mekong in many ways, Williams was perhaps better equipped than some of his comrades to endure and acclimatize himself to the harsh conditions of the Delta.

This e-book has so far related the stories of three brave men. James E. Williams is the fourth, and like the story of Captain Donlon that began this small volume, his story is the stuff of military legend. If a person did not know that James Williams had actually done what he did, they would think they were reading the script of, or watching, an action movie.

James E. Williams was cited for bravery many times. Among his decorations are: 3 Bronze Stars, Two Silver Stars, 3 Purple Hearts, Two Navy and Marine Corps Medals, two Legions of Merit, the Navy Cross...and the Medal of Honor. He received many other duty and service citations as well. Williams is the most decorated enlisted man in the history of the United States Navy. An Arleigh Burke class destroyer launched in 2003 bears his name.

Williams joined the Navy in 1947 at age sixteen. He saw service all over the world, including off the Korean peninsula during the Korean War. He served with distinction throughout his career. When he voluntarily went to Vietnam in 1966, he was a nineteen-year Navy veteran and did not have to go, James E. Williams went unfathomably above and beyond the call of duty.

Williams was assigned to River Patrol Force made up of PBR's and Swift boats, and often referred to as the "Brown Water Navy". Though on a larger vessel Williams would have been an important cog in the functioning of the ship, when he was assigned to the small boats of the River Patrol Force, he was given command of his own boat, PBR-105. The way Williams commanded the boat and put it into action, the enemy could not be blamed for thinking a destroyer had somehow made its way up river.

As it was, the PBR's were heavily enough armed for the jobs they were assigned to. The boats carried two .50 caliber machine guns, one .30 caliber medium machine gun, ship mounted grenade launcher, plus the personal weapons of the crew. Some crews changed the configuration of their boats' weaponry more to their liking, and yet others had other weapons added to them, for example flamethrowers adapted from tanks.

The thirty-one foot boats were capable of twenty-five or thirty knots powered by two two-hundred twenty horsepower engines. The crew complement was four men. Usual patrols consisted of two boats for mutual support, sometimes more depending on the mission. Patrols lasted from twelve to sixteen hours or more.

Recounting all of the actions that Williams played a part in and was cited for would take more space than available in this short e-book, but just recalling two will give the reader an idea of what kind of a man and sailor James Williams was.

The Mekong Delta was known to the forces of the United States as a hotbed of Viet Cong activity. One of the goals was to cut off supplies moving in and out of the Delta, and to prevent as many of the enemy as possible from leaving the area. Venturing into the area was a different story. In the preceding chapter, you read about Clarence Sasser, a medic in the 9th Infantry Division. For a time, the 9th was the only regular infantry unit that ventured into the Delta. To clear the Delta of all enemy forces would take an effort that would leave the forces of the United States vulnerable in other areas of the country and involve more casualties than it was already taking in what was becoming an unpopular war. So it was that units of the SEALs and other Special Forces units carried out very specialized and limited missions in the Delta, as did the men of the Brown Water Navy.

On July 23, 1966, Williams was the captain of PBR-105 on a mission to seize weapons, supplies and gather intelligence on the Cua Tieu tributary of the Mekong. Accompanying his boat was another US vessel, PBR-101 who was carrying the mission commander, and South Vietnamese forces.

Williams was directed to investigate a sampan close to shore for enemy personnel and weapons. As Williams maneuvered 105 under the light of a flare, the men on the sampan opened fire. Ordering his boat around to the best firing position, Williams opened fire on the enemy, killing six of the nine VC on board. The other three went over the side of the motorized sampan, which continued in circles. As he was making his way onto shore, one of the remaining VC opened fire on 105, which was circling the sampan close to shore, preparing to secure it with ropes and hooks. This man was also cut down by Williams. The other two men either drowned or made it into the forest on the banks. Williams secured the sampan. On board were weapons, maps and other intelligence. This action resulted in Williams' second Bronze Star. The first had been awarded three weeks before for similar coolness under fire in the destruction of a number of enemy boats and personnel in a heavily populated area of the Delta. That was Williams' first day in action. His third Bronze Star would also be awarded for action under the fire of the enemy. He earned the Navy and Marine Corps medal for rescuing men trapped aboard a US Navy dredge that had hit a mine in the Mekong in January 1967, the same month he would be awarded the Navy Cross.

One month later, Williams was in command of both PBR-105 and PBR-101 on a mission up the Mekong River. It soon became evident to Williams why it would take a concerted and heavy effort to remove the VC entirely from the forty thousand square mile delta area. On this patrol, Williams' boats came under fire from an estimated one hundred different gun emplacements along the banks of the wide river.

As the Americans returned fire, destroying or suppressing a number of VC gun positions, they noticed a motorized sampan in the distance. As they closed with it, fire from both banks of the river attempted to distract the Americans from the fleeing boat. This did not dissuade Williams, who closed and captured the sampan, its cargo, secret enemy documents, and the high-ranking VC aboard. For this action, Williams was awarded the Silver Star, the first of two. He was also awarded the Purple Heart for a wound to the face while pursuing the enemy craft.

On Halloween, 1966, Williams was again in command of a two-boat patrol looking for contraband on the Mekong when two of the sampans on the river nearby opened fire on 105. When the two PBR's returned fire, one of the enemy boats was torn to pieces, its crewman killed. The others high-tailed it into a nearly inlet. This was a dangerous place for Williams to go. Any number of hazards existed – shallow water, mines, and/or other obstacles, and of course, the enemy.

As Williams and the other PBR chased the enemy into the inlet, they almost immediately came under enemy fire from VC in almost invisible positions on both banks. The PBR's returned fire as they sped past the VC positions and out of range, but they soon came under even heavier fire when they came in range of seven more armed sampans and two of the larger "junks" that plied the river. "Junk" is a generic terms for a wooden commercial vessel in Asia that is usually anywhere between seventy and one hundred or so feet long, with some variation. A junk bristling with modern weapons was definitely a threat to Williams and his men. Not only were Williams and his comrades faced now with ten boats, but also heavy automatic weapons fire was coming from emplacements on shore. From the start when they pursued the enemy boat into the inlet until the end of the battle, three hours went by.

Over the course of the next couple of hours, Williams and the men under his command engaged the enemy while maneuvering at high speed to avoid serious damage to their vessels and themselves. To make him more easily heard and seen, Williams constantly exposed himself to the enemy. From various positions on his boat, he directed the fire and the route of the vessels under his command, all the while firing weapons of his own.

Realizing that the odds were greatly against his two boats, Williams radioed for air support from helicopter gunships based some miles away. While Williams waited for the helicopters to arrive, he drove deeper into enemy territory – at this point, it did not matter whether he went backwards or forwards, either way was teeming with VC on the banks and on the water.

Williams, his crew and his companions on the other PBR pushed resolutely up the inlet and in the process destroyed nearly sixty enemy vessels – sampans and junks of various sizes.

It was getting dark by the time the US gunships appeared. From his place on the water, Williams accurately directed the fire of the helicopters above. When it became fully dark, Williams took a risk and ordered his boats to turn on their searchlights to illuminate targets for both the gunships and the PBR crews. The result was the destruction of the enemy in the area. Sixty-five boats had been destroyed and hundreds of VC killed or wounded – most of them by the *eight* men of the two PBR's, Williams included. For this action, James Williams was awarded the Medal of Honor.

Williams had arrived in Vietnam in May 1966. By the end of October, he had won multiple Bronze Stars, the Silver Star twice, the Purple Heart, and the Medal of Honor. Five months.

However, Williams was not finished. On January 15 1967, Williams was operating in the Delta again, with a task force of other American vessels and South Vietnamese units. Again, he was the commanding officer of a three-boat PBR patrol. His assignment this time was to look for enemy troop's movements and supplies on another tributary river of the Mekong, the Nam Thon River. There was a suspected crossing route for sizable enemy forces and Williams' patrol was sent to investigate.

It was not long before Williams again interrupted the enemies' plans. He did indeed come across a major crossing route for the Viet Cong in the Delta area, and once again was taken under fire from enemy emplacements and soldiers on the banks of the river. Returning fire, Williams led his vessels out of the area to coordinate artillery and airstrikes on the enemy he had found, and to remove any chance of a "friendly fire" incident.

Strong air and artillery attacks pounded the area for some time, but it could not be assumed that the enemy force had been destroyed or even weakened. Williams had to go back in. When he did, his three boats were once again taken under heavy fire. As he had in October, Williams led from the front, exposing himself to enemy fire as he coordinated the efforts of the PBR's. Several enemy emplacements were destroyed and many of the Viet Cong enemy killed.

While the firefight was going on, Williams directed one of the PBR's to investigate a large sampan which he saw a distance away. As soon as this PBR headed towards the sampan, the enemy increased their fire – obviously, the enemy boat contained something of value. At this point, Williams ordered the sampan to be destroyed without investigation and his patrol to withdraw afterward. One problem – the third boat experienced temporary mechanical failure and was dead in the water for a time. While the crew repaired the vessel, Williams' boat and the other PBR provided both cover and covering fire for the stranded boat, which was soon back in operation. However, in the time it took to get back into action, James Williams was wounded again, this time seriously. Despite this, he continued to lead his force out of danger.

Nearly four hundred of the enemy had been trying to cross the river when Williams came upon them. Not only did Williams and his comrades prevent this, but they killed sixteen Viet Cong with many wounded, destroyed nearly a dozen enemy boats, a half dozen emplacements and more than a ton of the Viet Cong's main food supply – rice. For this action, Williams was awarded the Navy Cross. A few days later, he was awarded the Navy and Marine Medal mentioned in a previous paragraph. Williams *had been in Vietnam for just seven months.*

James E. Williams retired from the Navy that same year and was awarded the Medal of Honor by President Johnson in 1968. He went on to

become a U.S Marshal, where he retired. This hero passed on in 1999.

Chapter 5: The Extraction

Around November 1965, regular North Vietnamese Army divisions under General Vo Nguyen Giap began testing new weapons against the Americans on the battlefield. A significant number of troop casualties resulted and the commanders wanted to conduct a reconnaissance mission to gather details about the weapon's area of influence and consequently7 how to counter it. They utilized secret long-range patrol to ensure that the mission would have a great chance of success.

In December 1965, a team composed of four men was given the reconnaissance mission. They were the 5th Special Forces Group long-range reconnaissance unit, also referred to as Delta Project. One of these men was Charles McDonald. They were assigned to search an area for enemy activity but had no information about the target area. Under normal circumstances, it would be unwise to proceed. Since the situation makes it necessary to take a big risk, they had to commit to it. The team boarded a Huey helicopter the next day after their mission preparation and last-minute briefing.

The armed forces make use of a tactic called "false insertion" where they unload the troops at an area far from the actual insertion point to confuse the enemy. This will either have them believe that the false insertion was the actual area of operation (AO), or confuse them where the actual area of operation is. They made use of this tactic and dropped off south from the actual landing zone.

The helicopter's sound gradually became inaudible as it moved back towards the command center. At the same time, the sun was also starting to set behind the mountains. Charles and his team were on their way to the actual landing zone. By the time they arrived, there was only enough daylight left to find a suitable hiding spot for the night and make it inconspicuous to the enemy forces. They found a suitable thicket that had a layer of dry leaves on top of decomposing ones. Any object that would make any sound such as twigs was removed so that it won't make any noise when they are moving about. After setting up their spot for the night, they promptly reported to their command center of their successful arrival to the landing zone. The next situation report was scheduled at 730 AM, which meant it was time to mobilize.

The soldiers knew that they should forgo eating and smoking as it would make them sluggish and also give out their position due to strong odors. Charles being a non-smoker, knew that he had a keener sense of smell than the rest of the team. No matter how camouflaged their sleeping area was, the team knew that it was imperative to maintain alertness. He noticed that the forest was eerily quiet and that something didn't feel right.

His intuition was seemingly on point when he began hearing barks from a distance. Since the sound was faint, he and another team member brushed it off and assumed that it was just a barking deer that was native in the forests of Southeast Asia. Some time later, they were proven wrong. The barking did not come from just one animal. And definitely not from a barking deer. The barking came from several dogs from a nearby village. Charles looked at one of his team members, Bell, who was also wary of the danger. They knew that one dog barking was nothing to worry about. When several dogs bark simultaneously, it meant that several people were moving about. They decide to wait it out.

And hour passed and everything seemed to settle down Charles and Bell listened and waited. They were quite sure that something was coming because of the unusual silence around the forest.

A few minutes later, their fears were confirmed when they heard rustling and the sound of metal hitting metal. The thuds were unmistakably from humans. They had hoped that their insertion would not have alerted enemy forces about their mission, but now it appeared that wasn't the case. Bell woke the two other soldiers up in a non-alarming manner. All of them were now awake and on high level alert. They lay still and decided that the situation called for them to stay. However, should the situation escalate, they were prepared to make a run for it.

Even though there was a standby air forward controller on a distant base, he wouldn't be on-station until daytime. Air support and emergency extraction was not an option. The situation grew even tenser when there were sporadic firing of guns from different directions. They were close enough that they could see the muzzle flashes. However, that behavior simply indicated that the Vietnamese forces had no definite lead about their specific location. The gunshots and shouts were taunts so that Charles and the others would inadvertently give away their specific location. They also noted that the search party originally moved as one platoon, but eventually split into smaller groups scouring different areas. They were momentarily relieved when it became apparent that the enemies were not thorough enough with their search to scour the thicket they were in. They remained silent and calm until the noises died out. The search party called it off for the moment. It also meant that they didn't have to break into a run in the middle of the night.

A few hours past midnight, Charles noticed that Bell stiffened. He squeezed Bell's leg and asked in a hushed tone if he was awake. Bell responded quietly that he heard distinct sounds indicating that the enemies were on their trail again.

The team waited for 'Before Morning Nautical Twilight' (BNMT) to start mobilizing. This was the early morning time when there would be sufficient predawn light to be able to see one's immediate front. They could already see each others' faces and each one only reflected everyone's fears. They had hoped that the search had been called off but they knew it was just wishful thinking.

The soldiers noted that the search party didn't return from the way they came. This meant that the search party had surrounded the area and would be sweeping until their hiding spot was found. They needed to move as soon as they could because staying longer meant that they will be inevitably found, and being found meant certain death.

Before leaving their spot, they took a couple of salt pills each and drank water. They knew that they wouldn't have time to do so later, while on the move. They covered the hiding spot with dried leaves and carefully rearranged the brush to cover their tracks. Charles set his compass to night setting because he found it easier to read that way when on the run. Being found was no longer a question but a glaring certainty that they refuse to verbally acknowledge. Each one, however, knew what was impending and prepared themselves mentally.

It was already 7:00 AM, thirty minutes before the next scheduled situation report. They slowly crept out of the thicket one by one. They dropped to a crawl and moved on all fours since normal human movement is upright and it would be easy to distinguish one even in a dense forest. It also provided them with clear sight of the underbrush where they could easily see enemy movement. They moved about individually, spaced out about five meters from one another. Even the slightest crack of sticks and crushing leaves were avoided to maximize stealth. The fear that nipped at them all night long was now used in their favor. It provided them with increased awareness and critical decision-making skills. It was now the instinct of survival that provided them with the extra push they needed.

Charles directed the others to move eastward and after a set distance, head towards the north. Their guns were strapped in a way that it would not scrape the ground yet be combat-ready when going for a firing position. Behind Charles was Bell, who was creeping at a slightly higher eye-level. Once again, Charles noticed the unusually silent surroundings. Even the wind was unnervingly calm. Instinctively, they knew that the enemy was there.

At 7:30AM they took out their radio and proceeded with their scheduled situation report. They updated the command center with their current situation and were assured that helicopter crews are prepared to launch if needed. After the transmission, their radio operator unscrewed and folded the antenna, then placed it back into his bag. Bell tapped his rifle as a signal to continue their movement.

Right before they could cover a few meters, Charles noticed movement in the underbrush. The others took notice of it and all of them froze. Out of nowhere, about a dozen birds flew right past them as if fleeing from something. Then there was the silence again. They waited for several minutes while trying to figure out what startled the birds.

They looked at each other and agreed that they should switch their direction immediately. Charles checked his weapon and made sure it was ready to fire at a moment's notice. If it were an option, they would run. If cornered however, they will have to fight a very lopsided battle. It was not looking good because for him, it felt like they were crawling around a box. A box with guns closing in from all sides.

In an instant, the deafening silence of the forest was shattered by loud explosions of anti-personnel mines. The team was caught off guard by the blast and felt the full brunt of the shock wave. Although there was no direct hit from the mines, the blast temporarily disabled them from reacting. Even with the loud ringing in their ears, Charles could feel and somehow hear the bullets flying past them. With presence of mind, he disregarded the agonizing after-effects of the mine to determine where the bullets were coming from. The Vietnamese were hidden at the base of three empty anthills. He saw that there was very little cover between them and the Vietnamese forces. There was no other option but to move.

The other three were apparently back to their senses because Bell screamed "Grenade!" to instruct each of them to take one out. When Bell saw that they were all holding one, he signaled to have them simultaneously remove the pins and lob it into the direction of the enemies. Their grenades were on point and it obliterated the anthills. The shooting temporarily stopped and it was now the Vietnamese who were disoriented by the shock wave. Charles heard nervous chatters from the enemy's direction. They had to take the opportunity to make a run for it. At that point, camouflage did not matter anymore.

Charles found himself lagging behind his teammates. He increased his pace to close the gap to stay together as a unit. They moved into a dense part of the forest with slopes that demanded not only the strength and endurance of their legs but also their upper body. They kept running amidst flying bullets that the enemies were blindly firing into their general direction. One bullet found its way to a tree that was only a few inches from Charles's head. Bell was leading the run at a significant distance.

While Charles was slowly covering the distance between him and his teammates, he saw Bell get a direct hit into his rucksack, saving him from a bullet. Bell stumbled as the shot put him off balance. He immediately stood up and took off running once more. They crisscrossed trees while running to provide rear cover and cut direct line of sight from the pursuers. Bell fell again, this time not because or enemy fire, but because of slamming directly into a tree. All of them were starting to feel the toll of the physical demand. Their burst of running started to pay off as the shooting started to dwindle. Charles looked back and saw that there was no movement behind them. The others also noticed that they have given themselves and their pursuers a huge gap. They ran at a slower pace and so did Charles. They understood that to continue a blistering pace was not a good idea. Even though it would give them a significant lead from the pursuers, they will burn out sooner and they will be caught.

When Charles caught up with the others, he saw that they were setting up the radio to try and contact the Forward Air Controller. The folding antenna wouldn't come out so the radio controller took out a long antenna. Charles looked back and saw movement in the distance. They had to ditch their contact attempt and start running again.

After increasing the gap between them and the pursuers, they attempted another radio contact with the communications officer at the command center. Bell reported that they were in contact with the enemy forces and are trying to evade. Command center acknowledged their report, but gave them the bad news. There weren't any suitable extraction points near the team. However, they were given a general direction of where the nearest extraction may be done. They were also told that there were a couple of gunships on the way to provide air support if needed.

Once again, they picked up their pace and started running. Since they were in a dense forest, it was near impossible for air support to give them cover fire unless the team indicated their last locations when they made radio contacts with the communications officer. They deployed smoke grenades after every radio contact so that the air support can determine where they were and where the enemy will be presumable, since the Vietnamese were still in pursuit.

Charles was tasked with rear security. He was to check from time to time if there was any movement from behind that indicated nearby pursuers. He was to tap his rifle twice if he spotted anything. He noticed that every time he would spot a pursuer, it would always be the same person. It was the enemy's tracker, no doubt. Even though he wanted to turn back and kill the tracker, he decided against it because it would have closed the distance between him and the rest of the enemy forces. Their only choice now was to outlast their pursuers in a test of endurance.

At times, he could hear the gunships rain down bullets somewhere behind them. The air support did not seem to deter the Vietnamese. The consistent threat of the chase proved that they were very cunning and focused.

Finally, when the clearing for extraction was in sight, they were slightly relieved. Charles laid down among the tall grass just outside of the clearing, giving in to his exhaustion. He could hear the sound of the helicopter that was going to pick them up. His rest was fleeting and too early. Bell instructed him to go to the clearing and open his panel to signal the Huey. To Charles this meant that he was going to be out in the open, possible in full view of the Vietnamese. It felt like a death sentence. Still, it was necessary so that they could be located by the Huey and be promptly extracted. He ran into the open and opened his signal. Out of instinct and exhaustion, he immediately lay on the ground.

Bell and the others were making radio contact with the Huey to confirm their location. They were apparently successful as the helicopter slowly landed in the clearing. With the thought of imminent extraction, Charles was overwhelmed with a sense of relief and complacency. Bell prodded him to move because they still had pursuers and who were quickly closing the gap.

The helicopter took off with all four safely on board. Below them were visible muzzle flashes from Vietnamese forces who were still attempting to fire at them. This gave away their position and the accompanying gunships promptly fired at them back.

They were debriefed upon arriving at the base. After the ordeal, Charles wanted to treat himself to a hot shower and a cold beer. However, when their commander, Col. Charlie Beckwith asked him how he was doing, he responded nonchalantly that he was okay. He was then instructed to go back the next day.

Chapter 6: Survival Threshold

On May 27th, 1970, the North Vietnamese Army and Viet Cong bases in the border regions of Parrot's Beak, Angel's Wing, and Fishhook were devastated. Three weeks into the Cambodian raid of their bases, a significant number of enemy soldiers were killed and wounded. Tons of weapons, ammunition, and military stores were captured or destroyed. This assault left several stragglers from enemy troops scraping whatever they can, subjecting American troops to unpredictable guerrilla warfare.

In the Fishhook area, a five-man patrol were inside a wooded hilltop. The area overlooked grassy fields that Viet Congs used for farming. In the distance, the nearest American installation, Fire Support Base David, could be seen. It was constructed with makeshift materials and with hasty workmanship just to accommodate offensive movements that needed artillery support.

The troops on the hilltop came from Hotel Company, 75th Rangers First Cavalry Division Long-Range Reconnaissance Patrol. Their assigned mission to scout the area revealed very little as it was apparently totally abandoned by the Viet Congs. Although there were bunkers, trails, and farm plots, it looked like they did not intend to stay once the raid started.

However, they found it unusual that the crops in the farm plots were well tended. It seemed that the area was abandoned only very recently. The recon team also theorized that the Viet Congs tended to the crops until the last minute because they knew that American troops would be pulled out soon as there was already a public announcement of it. Once the troops are out, they would come scuttling back to still healthy crops. All the enemies needed to do was exercise a little bit of patience. Instinctively, they didn't take the theory as fact because they knew that the Viet Congs were spoiling for a fight after a humiliating assault of their bases.

Less than one hour from their extraction, the assistant team leader, Sgt. Erwin Thessin, spotted three North Vietnamese Army soldiers coming out of the woods at a distance from the hilltop's base. They could not have been mistaken for farmers as they were wearing floppy jungle hats, green fatigues with no insignia and rubber sandals. And the fact that they were carrying AK-47's.

The three were casually walking around and toward the hilltop while scanning the sky for American helicopters. It was yet unclear if they were aware of the LRRP's presence, but their actions were indicative that they had no idea of the LRRP's on the hilltop.

Sp.4 Lee Comstock, the team leader, brought his weapon up to a firing position. He waited until the enemy soldiers were well within accurate firing range and then he opened fire. Two of them were hit and fell to the ground. The third soldier returned fire and was apparently skilled enough that he gave his injured comrades time to crawl back into the woods. The enemies also used their packs as shields as they made their escape.

After the short encounter, Comstock instructed the team medic, Thessin, to cover the south part of the hill while the rear scout, Sgt. Chuck Donahoo was tasked to cover the north side.

Comstock and Thessin proceeded to check the packs left behind by the three North Vietnamese Army soldiers. The pool of blood close to the packs indicate that the two who were shot were severely injured. They secured ropes around the abandoned rucksacks to make sure that they weren't booby trapped. Although it was near impossible that the enemies could have rigged it in time, Comstock decided to act on the safe side. They got behind a cover in case of explosion. One by one they pulled the ropes and sure enough, they weren't rigged. Upon pulling the third rucksack however, they were greeted with the sight of a large group of North Vietnamese Army units coming from the forest. It was now clear that the three enemy soldiers were sent to scout the American forces situated on the hilltop.

At that moment, Donahoo was laying prone on the ground while diligently securing his area. Upon hearing the gunshots fired at Comstock and Thessin, he started to turn toward the area. Before he could do so, he was greeted with two North Vietnamese Army soldiers in front of him. They opened fire at Donahoo immediately and the rounds hit his weapon, throwing him backward. The two enemy soldiers were approaching fast and Donahoo saw that his weapon was a few feet away from him. Going after it would have given the enemy a clear shot. He decided to drop his rucksack and use it for protection. Then he pulled his back-up weapon, a grenade launcher. He fired a canister at the two approaching enemies and the explosion sent them flying. He fired a few more canisters at the enemy's direction until there was no more enemy presence in his front area.

Donahoo stood up and checked his wounds. He found three entry wound near his right ribs that were as big as his thumb. He then checked his back and concluded that there was no entry wound from any of the three shots. He wasn't bleeding much, but it worried him even more as it was an indication of internal bleeding. His right side of the body was starting to get numb and heavy. He used the dressing on his first aid pouch to temporarily cover his wounds. Upon noticing another enemy approaching, he let off another round and then turned toward Comstock and Thessin.

The wounded ranger fired explosive rounds toward the area of Comstock and Thessin's attackers. It gave the two enough cover fire to retreat. Comstock waved at Donahoo to follow them and fall back, but he was not aware of Donahoo's injuries. Thessin followed up Comstock's order and yelled for Donahoo to follow.

Pain was now starting to creep through Donahoo's body. The numbness was now turning into a burning sensation. He assessed his situation and decided that he had to formulate another plan because sprinting or even walking toward his teammates was impossible given his current state.

He spotted an anthill situated about midway and decided to crawl toward it, then take his time to crawl toward the team with the added cover of the mound. Every painful step and lunge he took finally led him to the anthill. He stood up to walk again, but the pain became too much to bear. He fell to the ground in pain.

Amidst the exchange of bullets in the air, Thessin pulled him up and helped him rise. The team, including Thessin provided cover fire until they joined the group. Thessin checked Donahoo's wounds and told him that he needed Medevac. Air support was on the way, but they needed to move to an appropriate spot where he could be loaded safely. Their current position would have made the helicopter and Evac team vulnerable to enemy fire.

Comstock coordinated with the gunships to determine target locations. The gunships cleared the path to the extraction point and kept the enemy forces at bay. They were successfully evacuated from the battlefield. The Medevac team immediately injected Donahee with morphine.

He was taken to a hospital and was wheeled off to surgery. He had lacerated liver and internal bleeding in the abdominal cavity. He also suffered broken ribs. He awoke several hours later in the hospital still groggy from the medications.

A few days later, Air Cavalry Division Commander Maj. Gen. George W. Casey presented Sgt. Chuck Donahoo with an Army Commendation medal, a Silver Star, and a Purple Heart. Gen. Casey spent a few more minutes talking with Sgt. Donahee personally and told him that he was proud that he was in his ranger division.

Chapter 7: Prison Raid

North Vietnamese Army prison camps lived up to their notoriety as places that reeked of misery and death. Allied forces who became prisoners of war would often prefer death than be locked into a cage and subjected to different kinds of torture, interrogation, and eventually death at the hands of their North Vietnamese captors. They were given minimal food while incarcerated, just enough sustenance to keep them alive and unwillingly cater to the sadistic needs of the Viet Congs.

The prison camps were also notorious for being well hidden even from the air. Usual prison camps were found in caves, dense forests, and mountainsides. The base of each makeshift prison cell was lined with wooden planks. They were constructed with vertical saplings spaced strategically to allow viewing from all sides, but not enough to allow the severely famished captives a way out. The cells were roofed with a thick layer of interwoven palm leaves and then covered by even more leaves on top that were carefully placed to provide camouflage. One can only imagine the prisoners' frustration every time one of the allied aircraft and helicopters fly by oblivious of their situation.

A handful of American soldiers was kept at the Tuy Hoa Valley, Phu Yen Province, around two hundred miles from Saigon in the north east direction. They were to relieve Korean Marines who were protecting Southern Vietnamese villagers, particularly the farmers. It was the annual rice harvest, so they had to secure the place because any sign of vulnerability would certainly be exploited by the North Vietnamese Army.

There were also reports that the 95th North Vietnamese Army Regiment situated themselves somewhere around the coastal side of the thickly forested mountains. The allied forces understood that the North Vietnamese Army was in control of the high ground and they were in control of the low ground.

In September 1966, a two North Vietnamese Army units walked into the base camp, calmly offering their surrender. When they were interrogated, they identified themselves the unit they belonged in. They proceeded to reveal that their unit had a prison camp at the side of the mountain where they held fifty prisoners. One was an American soldier, two were Korean Marines, and the rest were South Vietnamese soldiers and villagers. He claimed that there was a total of 50 prisoners in the said prison camp.

The elicited information was immediately relayed to the base camp's commanding officer, Col. Meinzen. He decided to act as quickly as possible to increase the possibility of extracting as many living prisoners as possible. It was also prudent to act fast to minimize the chances of the enemy forces getting wind of an impending rescue operation. One of the captive North Vietnamese volunteered to lead the way to the prison camp location.

One platoon was on the north side of the valley. They were updated with the unexpected development at the base camp. They were briefed and instructed to take the troops across the valley rendezvous with Tiger Force, the Brigade's short-range reconnaissance element. Upon hearing that the information was given by North Vietnamese with little interrogation in addition to offering to lead the way, they were almost certain that it was going to be an ambush. They felt that even their commanding officer knew the likelihood of it as a trap, but probably felt that the decision made was the best suited for the current situation. They just had to prepare for it with different countermeasures should the plan go awry. Although the troop members just came from a recent encounter with North Vietnamese Army soldiers, they accepted the mission with no sign of protest.

It was almost sundown when they set out for the rendezvous with Tiger Force. They cautiously trekked across the valley. The majority of the covered terrain were rice fields. Although their position was very vulnerable for an attack, they had prior intelligence information that North Vietnamese Army presence in the area was unlikely. Still, they did not let their guard down and still kept a high level of alertness. When darkness finally crept over the sky, they decided to set a defense perimeter in a narrow canyon. Before setting up, however, they made a sharp change in direction in order to confuse the enemies in case they were being followed. They attempted to establish communication with Tiger Force to update their locations and the respective distance from the rendezvous point. They weren't successful in the attempt and finally decided to settle into their defense perimeter.

When the first sign of light came at dawn, they were already awake. It was the time Viet Congs usually preferred to attack. They lay among the tall grass and kept themselves hidden until the sun peered over the mountains. It was the mountain where the alleged North Vietnamese Army is located.

They stood up from the grassy hiding place and were surprised to see that the unit that they were to rendezvous were less than a hundred meters away from their location. Apparently, they had set their defense perimeters close to one another with no knowledge of the other unit's proximity. Had there been any North Vietnamese Army units that stumbled between their locations the night before, they would have been at a great disadvantage.

The two forces completed the link-up and continued toward their objective. After a few minutes, they arrived at the base of the mountain. They considered the possibility that if there were any watchers on top, they would have already been seen and thus must proceed with extra caution. Tiger Force led the way. Eventually they came upon a field of abandoned mines. They sent scouts to scour for any deadly devices. It took them quite some time to finally determine a clear path for the rest of the unit. Once they were safely through the fields, they were now right in the heart of the enemy territory.

They came upon a high speed trail that was apparently used often. They decided to use it to speed up their advance toward their objective. The chances of rescuing more prisoners would increase if they went faster. Their North Vietnamese prisoner serving as their guide nodded to confirm that taking that path takes them to the right direction.

While walking up the trail, they were expecting enemy forces to come out from the wood lines and start open firing at their group. The lack of enemy presence was making the troops believe that they were walking into a well planned ambush.

Only silence greeted them as they continued their climb. Suddenly, the column stopped. Tiger Force's designated point element spotted a seemingly abandoned outpost in a cave a little bit further ahead. Once they have confirmed that it was indeed empty, they went back to the trail, and continued onward. The column stopped again as another outpost came into view. Once again, Tiger Force sent a point element to scout the area. Out of the tense and silent surrounding came a loud gunshot. The outpost happened to be manned by several guards, one of them was shot by the point element. At this point, they knew that other North Vietnamese Army forces nearby heard the shot. It alerted them of the allied troops' presence.

They had to move fast so they hurried along the trail or else the enemies might execute the prisoners. Late afternoon, the trail finally ended. It only meant that they had already reached their destination. They scanned the area and found the makeshift prison cells. They fell silent upon seeing the prisoners inside. They were emaciated and looked close to death. The prisoners looked at the allied troops passively with sunken eyes. Any sense of relief would never have shown in their near-vegetative state. They spotted mounds near the prison cells, which were obviously buried bodies of prisoners who were killed. At the state that the living prisoners were in, the dead ones seemed to be the ones who are lucky.

Most of the prisoners were gone. The briefing stated that there would be around 50 but they were only able to spot eight. Suddenly, they heard hurried voices conversing in Vietnamese. The troops immediately knew that the captors caught wind of their approach and had started to move them to another location. The eight prisoners left would have slowed down the enemy's movement had they been brought along. Their joints were swollen, emaciated from extreme starvation, and evacuating them was not an option that the North Vietnamese considered. As to why they didn't shoot them before leaving, the allied troops can only speculate. Perhaps time was very crucial and they focused on taking the able prisoners. Perhaps they wanted to leave an impression onto the rescuers about the horrors of being their captive. The actions of the North Vietnamese forces in the camp washed away their suspicions of the guide setting them up for an ambush. Clearly, they were not expecting company.

The enemy voices started to fade and were already a good distance away from the allied troops. They went in pursuit, wanting to catch up to the North Vietnamese forces before dark. Each of them knew of the huge danger in pursuing the North Vietnamese forces. They knew all the best places to set up an ambush. At any time during their movement, they could have positioned several of their men in perfect hiding spots. The allied troops moved silently while staying as close to the bushes as possible. That way, the enemies will have a harder time locating them.

After a significant distance was covered, one soldier signaled to the others that something was wrong. He was looking at the bushes and noticed a slight rustling of leaves. His weapon was at the ready. Out of the thick bush, a prisoner fell down to the ground. From the looks of it, the prisoner was a woman. The soldier could have instinctively shot her in a wrong split-second decision. The enemy forces probably left the prisoner because she was slowing them down. She might have looked better than the other eight back at the prison camp, but it appeared that she had just became a burden to the fleeing Viet Congs.

They approached the prisoner cautiously as the enemies might have planted her as a bait. They also discovered that the prisoner was a Vietnamese. When they were certain that the prisoner wasn't placed as a trap, one trooper was instructed to take her back to the encampment.

The darkness was now creeping in and it became apparent that they would not be able to catch up to the fleeing enemies and the prisoners. The platoon made a very difficult decision to abandon the current objective and join Tiger Force back at the encampment. When they got back, they gathered their rations and handed them to their medic. The medic proceeded to distribute the rations to the liberated prisoners.

Troop members were assigned to carry the prisoners on their backs while they tried to cover more ground to distance themselves from the danger of intercepting North Vietnamese forces. They dropped off into a dry creek bed through an inconspicuous path. Going back to the trail would have been predictable and the enemy forces may have been expecting it. They followed the creek bed until they came upon a limestone overhand that would provide them with a shelter that needed minimal setup. They decided to settle in as it was getting too dark to continue. The rescued prisoners also needed to rest up and gather some strength to be able to make it back to the allied base camp.

As soon as daylight greeted the troops, they packed up quickly. They stayed close to the creek bed until they came to the narrow canyon where they previously set up a perimeter and linked up with Tiger Force.

They went through the canyon until they arrived near the edges of the rice fields and open grasslands of the Tuy Hoa Valley. They had been walking without acknowledging the danger of North Vietnamese pursuers. To them, the mission objective was now to get the rescued prisoners to safety and necessary medical interventions. Although there was a looming threat of an attack, they were going to have to deal with the situation the moment it presents itself. There was no particular battle plan given to it.

The relatively fast trek and absence of any enemy encounter brought them safely to the extraction zone. Medevac helicopters arrived and loaded the rescued prisoners. Once back to base camp, the platoon was not greeted with any thanks. Not even commendations for a job well done. All of them were back to their units and they were alive and safe. For them, that fact was enough to give them recognition from the mission. Unspoken among the platoon members was the disappointing fact that each one of them felt that they were responsible to some degree that only a few prisoners were liberated. Perhaps any commendation would be misinterpreted as sarcasm about how the mission turned out to be categorically a failure.

Some time later, they were told that one of the prisoners succumbed to his emaciated condition and passed away. They were also informed that he was a former Viet Cong who was captured by his former comrades. Naturally, he was subjected to harsher methods of torture.

Years after the platoon leader Charles McDonald retired from service, he was contacted by relatives of soldiers who were missing in action. He contacted a person of influence who was working at the Pentagon and told him of a prison camp location that may hold the key to finding some soldiers who were missing in action (MIA). He pointed out the location on a map and encircled the area with a pencil. His acquaintance browsed the archives in a filing cabinet and took out a portfolio that held the report for that particular mission. The file indicated that the sole American force who participated in the mission was the Tiger Force. As frustrating as it was to him, he had no means to contest what the file indicated.

A couple of months later, his acquaintance called and confirmed that it was verified through channels that there was indeed a prison camp at the given location. There wasn't any additional information given. He had to face the fact that that's how far the information would take him. Just the simple acknowledgment of the camp's existence. For some reason, possibly political, there was no follow through. Like most issued that didn't involve big political and military figures, it was swept under the rug.

Opportunity presented itself once more when Charles met another acquaintance who was serving on the Joint Casualty Resolution Team (JCRT). The friend laughed it off and accused him of fabricating a war story. Months later, that very acquaintance wrote to him and offered him a job at the Joint Casualty Resolution Team on the condition that he would renounce the methods used by Special Forces personnel to rescue prisoners of war. Defeated and frustrated, he lamented about how the government failed to take care of its armed forces.

Chapter 8: Behind Friendly Lines

In 1965, John Larsen was assigned at an interceptor site in Tay Ninh at Trang Sup. It was his first assignment. The camp was specializing in communication intelligence, but only the camp's A-teams were privy to that information. It would not have been prudent for all the camp's residents to know the true function of their base.

The reason for this is because John and the rest of the A-Team knew that a significant number of Vietnamese in the camp were sympathizers to the North Vietnamese Army. They also acknowledged the fact that some of them were highly efficient intelligence agents.

The camp was stacked with weapons and ammunition that regular soldier had no knowledge of. The cache of armaments were to serve as defense should the Vietnamese Army sympathizers grow in number and decide to overpower allied personnel. However, the cache did not reassure intelligence agents. It would take a simple grenade thrown at agents converging in a bunk to severely damage communications and security.

A routine procedure of the camp was to patrol a wood line some few kilometers away from the camp. They would always do the patrol quickly because a spy back at the camp would signal the North Vietnamese Army in the mountains. They never found out who was doing it.

John used to sleep in the dispensary of the camp. He adopted a camp mascot for added security measure. John would sneak some extra food to a dog they called "Old Yeller". He supposedly hated the Vietnamese. It was unusual in comparison to the other camp dogs because their actions were opposite of Old Yeller's. They would continuously bark at Americans for days until they get accustomed to the presence of that particular personnel. One evening, John awoke to a low growl. He saw Old Yeller intently looking at a particular direction. He got up and patted the dog. Old Yeller seems to have understood that they were to proceed stealthily. Down a small hallway, they found a man attempting to send Morse code that John assumed was probably for Nui Ba Den. The soldier held a small red flashlight believing that it was not bright enough to attract unwanted attention to what he was doing. John promptly stuck the muzzle of his M-14 behind the man's right ear and walked him toward the team house to be dealt with accordingly.

Sometimes, they would find .50 caliber machine guns with the feeding tray ajar. Upon closer inspection, they would find a variety of items, usually dirt, stuffed into the barrels. Another clincher was an incident that happened in August of 1967.

After being hospitalized for ten months due to tuberculosis and spending six more months retraining, John arrived in Pleiku eager to get back to work. They found out that the camp barber was carrying blasting caps. They investigated further and were surprised to see that the hollow barber chair made of plywood was filled with C4 plastic explosives. The barber shop was located behind the camp commander's office.

In another incident, a forklift operator spotted a thin wire running into what appeared to be a cluster of explosives. It was very fortunate because it happened during night time where it would be very difficult to spot a thin wire. The rig was inspected and sure enough, it was carefully placed explosives and were set to detonate on command.

The day after, a camp Sargent was met with a terrifying experience. He woke up to the alarm going off and just as he normally would, stated to put on his gear. He noticed that there was a slight pull on his shoulder as he leaned forward. He then checked why and noticed that there was a string that was attached to his shirt. His eyes followed the string to where its other end is located. At the other end there was a grenade. Fortunately, the pin was damaged and bent that the slight tug was not enough to pull it out. John noted how the Sargent should have locked away his gear to prevent similar setups.

There was no question about it. The camp integrity was not solid. Some were caught, some got away with it. Some little acts of terror were successful, some were not. Although the Viet Cong sympathizers might have been planning for a big takeover using minor acts of terror mounting up to a big climax, it was probably thwarted thanks to the efforts of the observant and extremely cautious A-teams (there were two) assigned at the camp.

Chapter 9: Both Sides of the War

When Americans look back at the Vietnam War, they think of a conflict in the mid to early sixties to the early 1970's that was the source of great unrest in the nation and which even today, forty years or so later, is the subject of great debate. Should the United States have even become involved in the war? Did we win battles and lose the war? Did the war and the intrigue involved with it help destroy Americans' faith in government? These and many more questions are still being asked and answered.

In Vietnam, the answer is quite clear cut. To many Vietnamese in the north and in the south, the war was one of independence, akin to the American Revolution. Though many people in the former South were opposed to communism, the idea of an independent Vietnam was something they had dreamed about for a long time.

For the Vietnamese, the war did not last one decade. In actuality, there had been an independence movement in Vietnam since its takeover by the French in 1887 after two decades of conflict. That fight was interrupted by another guerrilla war. This time the fight was against the Japanese from 1940-45. When that conflict ended and the French moved back in to reclaim their former colony, the Vietnamese went to war again. In the mid-50's, the nation had been divided into two, the communist North and the ostensibly democratic South, led by Emperor Bao Dai and a series of corrupt politicians/generals.

When the North Vietnamese continued to organize and supply communist guerrillas in the South, the United States became deeply involved which eventually led to the escalation of the conflict into a full-blown war involving over 500,000 US troops. Not until 1975 was Vietnam a united nation.

Even after the war with the United States, the Vietnamese found themselves in conflict: first with the bizarre and genocidal regime of Pol Pot in Cambodia, and against Cambodia's giant ally, and Vietnam's ancient enemy, China. The Vietnamese toppled Pol Pot, and though China could have brought the full force of its giant military to bear in Vietnam, the losses they sustained in the short border conflict dissuaded them from doing so.

To put it briefly, in the 20th century, despite losses greater to them than to their enemies, the Vietnamese fought and/or defeated the Japanese, the French, the Americans and the Chinese (as well as the Cambodians) in the span of thirty years, and emerged as an independent nation. Behind much of this fight and much of the strategy was a Vietnamese national hero, General Vo Nguyen Giap. It is with his story that we begin.

These coming chapters should in no way be taken as an endorsement of communism, nor be seen as pro-North Vietnam or Viet Cong, both of whom were guilty of serious atrocities. Its purpose is to give you another point of view.

Chapter 10: Giap

Vo Nguyen Giap was born in 1911 at the height of the second great wave of European Imperialism. He passed away at 102 years of age in 2013. In his lifetime, Vietnam went from a colonial backwater to a rising modern power whose military was respected around the world for its toughness and resilience. While reading these stories please note that in Vietnam, as in much of the Far East, a person's given name is written last but used as the main form of address.

Giap was born at a time when Vietnam was a nation consisting mostly of rural peasants and coastal fishermen. A number of cities lined the coast, but with the exception of two, Saigon in the south and Hanoi in the north, most Vietnamese cities were relatively small outposts dissipating slowly into the surrounding countryside. Even the Imperial city of Hue (pronounced "way") on the central coast was a small provincial city in 1911. Though the Vietnamese emperor remained on the throne, he was a symbol only – the French allowed him to remain, but without power.

For most of the world, the name "Vietnam" did not even exist. In 1911, the nation we now know as Vietnam was part of the larger French territory of French Indochina, which consisted of the modern nations of Laos, Cambodia and Vietnam.

Vietnam itself was divided into three administrative regions ranging from north to south: Tonkin, Annam and Cochin-China. Giap was born in the central region of Annam in Quang Binh province, and it was there that the formative events of his life took place.

The first was the death of his father, Vo Quang Diem. In 1919 the elder Vo was arrested by the French for subversive activity against their rule. This was likely true. Giap's father had taken part in previous uprisings against the French in the late 1880's. Held in notoriously bad conditions, Vo Quang Diem died while incarcerated.

To make matters worse, Giap's elder sister was soon arrested by the French as well. She died shortly after her release. Before he was ten years old, Giap had lost two members of his family to French maltreatment.

Giap's father had been a minor local official, and had received a formal education, which was a rarity in the Vietnam of the 19th century. Giap's education began as a young boy under his father's tutelage. After his father's death, relatives recognized Giap's intelligence and he was sent to school. This was not a common occurrence in the early 20th century either. Within two years, Giap was enrolled in a school administrated by the French in the nearest large city, the Imperial capital of Hue. The school, while under French oversight, was founded and run by a Catholic Vietnamese named Ngo Dinh Kha, and was attended by three men who would play central roles in the Vietnam of the future.

The first was Ngo Dinh Diem (1901-1963), the son of the school's founder. He would later become the President of South Vietnam and a bitter enemy of the Vietnamese communists and Giap. Diem would be South Vietnam's president until he began to lose control of the nation in 1963 amid religious and popular riots against his rule, and which were partially instigated by the North Vietnamese. Diem was assassinated by CIA operatives and replaced with another man thought to be more pliable to American wishes and aims. And another, and another...

The second of Giap's new acquaintances at the school was a young man named Pham Van Dong (1906-2000) who served as head of both North Vietnam (after the retirement of Ho Chi Minh) and the united nation of Vietnam after wars' end.

The third and most important of Giap's new acquaintances was a man named Nguyen Sinh Cung. This name was changed by tradition to Nguyen That Than ("Nguyen the Accomplished") by his proud father as a young man. Later in life when he began to publicly write and speak of Vietnamese independence, he took the name Nyugen Ai Quoc ("Nguyen the Patriot"). History knows him by his war name "Ho Chi Minh", or "He who has been enlightened", the man who led the Vietnamese independence movement against the French and much of the fight against the United States.

Giap (center) w/ Ho (center left) and Truong Trinh (later Communist
Party Secretary) and Central Committee member and future
diplomat Le Duc Tho (right) in 1948 during the war with France

Finding a political root in his anti-French feelings, Giap took part in protests against French rule and eventually was expelled from school for his part in the protests and his outspoken desire for Vietnamese independence. Back home after his expulsion, he joined a revolutionary movement which espoused independence and where he was introduced to communism.

In the late 1920's he returned to Hue, the center of Vietnamese political life at the time, and formed relationships with other like-minded young men and women. Giap did not join the Communist Party of Vietnam until 1931, after he had been working chaotically for independence for some time.

Though in the mind of Ho Chi Minh, who spent much of the 1920's and 30's overseas in France and the Soviet Union, communism was the model on which an independent Vietnam should be based, it should be remembered that at their core, the Vietnam Wars against the French and the United States were wars for independence and unification, with communism taking second place. There is no doubt that most of the men and women who took part in the wars were dedicated, even fanatical communists but they were Vietnamese first. This is witnessed by the subsequent war and poor relations to this day with China after the unification and the falling out with the Soviet Union in the mid-late 1980's.

In the 1930's Giap went to university in Hanoi where he studied law. He failed the equivalent of the bar exam due to the amount of time he spent in underground political activity. To earn a living, he became a history teacher. It was during this time that Giap was first truly exposed to the ideas of the military men and strategists that he would incorporate into North Vietnamese military strategy in the near future: the classic Chinese tactician and strategist Sun Tzu, Napoleon Bonaparte and the British commander who had won such fame in WWI, T.E Lawrence (better known as "Lawrence of Arabia").

During the 1930's the French regime in Indochina was a mirror of French politics at home – sometimes lenient towards left wing ideology, and sometimes not. However, by 1940 fear of both Hitler and Stalin in Europe was reflected in the French cracking down on hard-core communists at home and in their colonies after the German and Soviet dictators reached the accord of late summer 1939. Giap, Ho Chi Minh and other leading communists went into exile in China in the spring of 1940. Giap left behind a wife and child. His wife was to die in prison for revolutionary activity in 1943.

When France fell to the Germans in 1940, its far flung colonies either came under the control of the collaborationist Vichy French regime or the Free French government in exile. The colonies of Southeast Asia remained under the control of the Vichy regime, but were occupied by Germany's ally Japan in 1940. Japan allowed the Vichy French to govern the day to day affairs of the territory under Japanese direction. Now Vietnam was occupied by two foreign powers, and men like Ho Chi Minh and Giap knew from what was happening under Japanese rule in other areas that the occupation of their homeland was going to be even worse than it had been before.

Accordingly, under the leadership of Ho Chi Minh, the "Vietnamese Independence League" was formed to fight the occupation. This organization is best known by the shortening of its Vietnamese title – the "Viet Minh". Having experience in the organization of an underground political party, Giap was put in charge of organizing political activity in the China-Vietnam border area.

While in China, the Vietnamese and especially Giap, had come in contact with the Chinese communists under Mao Zedong. By 1940, the exploits of Mao and the Chinese Communist Red Army were legendary among communist revolutionaries. Having survived the thousand mile "Long March" of 1935-36, fighting and evading the forces of the Chinese Nationalists, the communists under Mao had established a large base at Yanan in central China from which they carried out a guerrilla war against the both the Nationalists and the Japanese. The tactics of the Chinese under Mao would be the model by which the Vietnamese would fight the Japanese and the French.

First they needed an army. To do this, Giap needed to return to Vietnam personally. For two years Giap and a small cadre of men worked in the mountain highlands of northern Vietnam.

One would be hard pressed to come up with a more perfect place for a hideout and base of operations than the highlands of northern Vietnam as you can see from the picture below:

Mountainous valleys like the one pictured above, river gorges, deep and thick forests and jungle in an ever changing climate that can run from hot and exceedingly humid to chilly and wet in a matter of a few hundred meters, the highlands of northern and central Vietnam were tailor-made for guerrilla war.

For those readers outside of Vietnam and Southeast Asia, it may also come as a surprise that many of the early supporters of the Viet Minh were not Vietnamese, at least not ethnically. Today, both northern and southern Vietnam is 85% ethnically Vietnamese. The other fifteen percent of the population consist of a variety of different ethnic groups and tribes, many of whom speak their own language and dialect. Many of the first people to join the Vietnamese communists under Ho and Giap were members of mountain tribes such as the Nung or Man Trang. One of the first obstacles that Giap and the others with him had to face was that of language, and initially much of the communication between the two groups was done with a primitive sign language and symbols/pictures. Communication was aided by the fact that Giap was linguistically gifted, learning French, Chinese and now the dialects of the mountain people.

Most of the first two years of their stay in the highlands was dedicated to winning over both Vietnamese and other locals to their cause, establishing an intelligence network to report on the French and Japanese, and distributing propaganda. Primitive schools were established in the highlands by the Communists, teaching local people both the basics such as reading and writing and also communist political theory and Vietnamese history.

By the summer of 1944, the Viet Minh had a wide sphere of influence in the Chinese border region and had established small cells within some of the larger villages and cities of the region. In the winter of 1944, it was decided that it was time to begin military action against the Vichy French and Japanese.

One of the first tenets of guerrilla warfare is to strike when and where it is least expected. It was decided that the first attack would take place on Christmas Day, 1944. French troops would be celebrating the holiday. They estimated that the soldiers would most likely be demoralized from being so far from home and/or drunk, and poorly trained and motivated Vietnamese colonial troops would be on duty.

Even this was risky. The Vietnamese force consisted of thirty four men and women, half of whom were armed with breech loading weapons from the late 19th century. The man who planned and led the attack was Vo Nguyen Giap.

The first Viet Minh attacks were on two small frontier outposts and were successful. Two French officers were killed and a number of Vietnamese colonial soldiers were taken prisoner and/or converted to communism. Perhaps more importantly, modern weapons and ammunition were captured as well. This was the pattern for a number of attacks that took place in winter 1944 and spring 1945. In one of these attacks, Giap was wounded in the leg, but soon recovered.

With the collapse of German resistance in France and the fall of the Vichy government, the Japanese removed all Vichy officials from what power they had left. In their place, the Japanese put the lineal Vietnamese emperor, Bao Dai (1913-1997). Bao Dai, who had been a brief college classmate of Giap, had no power and was seen during the war and afterwards to be a puppet of whatever foreign power would allow him to retain his title and way of life. First the French, then the Japanese, the French again and lastly the Americans.

With the French temporarily out of the picture the Viet Minh turned their attention to the Japanese. Though most believed the Japanese were eventually going to be defeated, no one was sure how long it would take. With this in mind, the sizable Japanese force in Vietnam remained a threat to the very end of the war. The Viet Minh, wanting their voices to be heard at any post-war international conference, began to stage hit and run attacks against the numerous Japanese outposts in the hinterlands of the country. One of their main goals was to seize as many Japanese weapons as possible, primarily artillery. In their raids, they were aided by Japan's primary enemy, the United States. This aid came in the form of small arms and officers and men from the Office of Strategic Services (the forerunner of the CIA) to train the Vietnamese in their use. This training would come back to haunt the Americans in the 1960's.

When WWII ended, the Vietnamese expected that their nation would be freed from French rule. After all, much of the rhetoric of the Allies, and of their Free French compatriot, General Charles DeGaulle, was about freedom and self-rule. However, like the Great War fought in 1914-1918, self-rule and freedom meant one thing for Europeans and entirely another for those who were not.

While Ho Chi Minh. Giap and the Viet Minh who now numbered in the thousands marched into Hanoi to form a new Vietnamese government with Ho at its head and Giap as Interior Minister, the Big Three powers met at Potsdam outside of Berlin after the end of the European war. It was there that Vietnam's fate was decided.

Joseph Stalin, Britain's new Prime Minister Clement Atlee and President Harry Truman came to the conclusion that the nation would be temporarily divided between the Nationalist Chinese under Chiang Kai-shek and the British, who would be acting on behalf of their French allies. Once the Western war ended and the French under DeGaulle had had time to re-organize, the British would hand power in Vietnam over to them.

At this point in time, the Viet Minh were in no condition to wage war against the Chinese and the British, and hoped that war-weariness and the rhetoric of freedom emanating from Western capitals would allow them to attain their goals without war.

In the time between the Japanese surrender in August and the late fall, Ho, Giap, and the Vietnamese communists had established themselves as the government in Hanoi. This brief period of self-rule was limited at best, and outside of Hanoi and the immediate area, Ho's influence was limited. By early fall tens of thousands of Nationalist Chinese and British had arrived in the north and south of the country. In late 1945, the first French troops began to arrive and the southern part of Vietnam was handed over to them by the British. The following spring, the French slowly moved into the north as well, and the Chinese began to depart.

For six months in 1946, the Vietnamese leadership was involved in talks with the French in Paris. A number of factors doomed these talks to failure. First and foremost was the French desire to regain her former position as a great power after the defeats of WWII. Another factor was Giap and measures he took within Hanoi which caused France and the Western Powers much consternation.

While Ho Chi Minh was in Paris attempting to negotiate Vietnamese independence, Giap was left in charge in Hanoi. He began to attack non-Communist Vietnamese nationalist groups in Hanoi, closing newspapers and imprisoning/killing their leaders. Rival Vietnamese factions fought each other in Hanoi's suburbs, with the communists coming out on top. More importantly, Viet Minh and the newly arriving French troops were involved in running skirmishes throughout the country.

These actions and events only fed the non-communist attitudes of Britain and the United States. In the end, France which was having its own post-war problems with communism, really never intended to allow Vietnamese independence. This was just as they refused to allow the independence of their African colonies. Giap's actions, designed to show the French that the Vietnamese had the capability to resist, doomed any chance of a peaceful settlement.

As they moved back into northern Vietnam, the French seized control of the largest port city in the country, Haiphong. The city was also key to the efforts of the Viet Minh in bringing in arms and other supplies to the north. Continual skirmishes and incidents between the French police and army and the Viet Minh escalated and in October, the local French commander took the fateful step of ordering the naval bombardment of Haiphong. This action, which caused thousands of Vietnamese casualties, made it certain that a peaceful resolution to the problems in Vietnam would not be reached. Returning from France after the fruitless talks there, Ho Chi Minh declared a state of war between the Viet Minh and France.

The first step in this war was a retreat. Giap, Ho, and the others knew that the Viet Minh were not then capable of taking on the French in Hanoi or almost anywhere else. They moved back into the northern highlands to the bases from which they fought the Japanese.

In many ways, the war known to Americans as the Vietnam War began in 1946. From the moment that Ho declared war on the French in 1946 until 1975, the northern Vietnamese and their sympathizers in the south fought continually. First against France with much American aid and then against the United States directly.

For the first two years of the Franco-Vietnamese War, the Viet Minh were limited in what they could do in their struggle. The primary problem was that of weapons and supply. Lack of weapons, not lack of manpower was the most pressing difficulty. The French had stockpiles of weapons from the war in Europe and from the United States. The Viet Minh had to rely on captured and/or smuggled weapons, both which were in limited supply.

There was one important element of war that the Viet Minh in the north did not lack, manpower. The rising world influence of the Soviet Union and in 1949 China attracted many to communism. So did Viet Minh propaganda, but the behavior of the French and the long held desire of the Vietnamese for independence provided even more. The Viet Minh spent the first two years training and conducting the same kind of small hit and run raids that were successful against the Japanese and Vichy French during WWII, and avoiding the many traps set by the French to wipe them out.

In the initial phases of the war, much of the French force consisted French colonial troops who were commanded by French officers and some non-coms, from North and Central Africa, Cambodia, and Laos. Many of the African troops were hardened veterans of the Free French campaigns in North Africa, Italy, and Europe, and had no experience as occupiers. For many of these troops, duty in Vietnam was a license for looting, rape and murder.

The one formation that consisted mostly of Europeans was the French Foreign Legion. Some of these troops were veterans of the British army who had been demobilized after the war and could find no home outside the armed forces. Many Foreign Legionnaires were Spanish fascists and a significant number were former German Wehrmacht and Waffen-SS troops. Many of the recruits had something in their past, many times a criminal history, that they wished to put behind them. Joining and surviving years in the Legion guaranteed French citizenship and a new identity. The Legion too had its share of nasty habits. These many incidents provided more recruits for the Viet Minh and fodder for communist propaganda.

The situation in Vietnam changed radically in 1949 with the victory of the Chinese Communists in their nations' civil war. With the end of war in China, the Chinese were free to provide weapons to their communist brothers to the south. Additionally, the opening of China allowed transports of weapons and supply from the Soviet Union to begin to trickle in as well.

The communist Chinese also provided advisers who helped direct and plan Viet Minh actions. Years of guerrilla warfare had made them expert, and Giap had studied both their campaigns and Mao Zedong's writing on tactics and political warfare.

By early 1950 Giap believed his forces strong enough to challenge the French in open battle. Coming down towards Hanoi from the Chinese border area, the Viet Minh inflicted a series of defeats against French forces in isolated outposts, and harassed their retreat towards Hanoi the Red River Delta area. Both sides sustained losses, but the Viet Minh gained influence over much territory and more importantly, seized stockpiles of heavy weapons and ammunition from the French outposts. This campaign took nearly a year, but when it was over, two important things had happened: much of northern Vietnam fell under Viet Minh control, and the French realized that they were in for a much bigger fight than they expected. Accordingly, they began to send sizable reinforcements to the region.

The French had retreated towards Hanoi and the Red River delta area

Vietnam - north of Hue lies the "Demilitarized Zone" (DMZ) which separated North and South Vietnam

on the Vietnamese coast. There it was easier to reinforce and resupply – and they could do this while protected by the guns of their navy. Here French fortunes began to change, temporarily.

Feeling that he had the French on the run, and controlling much of the countryside of northern Vietnam outside Hanoi, Giap, and the leadership of the Viet Minh bolstered by supplies from China, the USSR, as well as captured French weapons embarked on a series of conventional attacks at the beginning of 1951.

These attacks were a Vietnamese failure and illustrated to Giap that his forces were not ready to undertake a classic military campaign against a major power. Giap himself also learned some valuable lessons, and the seemingly careless way he threw Viet Minh forces at heavily defended French positions brought criticism on the part of some in the leadership.

In the battles of the Red River Delta, the Viet Minh lost nearly 20,000 men. The fighting took place in villages and open territory where the Vietnamese troops had little experience and the French much. Additionally, much of the fighting was against the French Foreign Legion, whose reinforced brigades were made up of heavily armed and highly motivated and trained soldiers. The French commander, General deLattre was a highly experienced and decorated WWII veteran who seemed one step ahead of Giap for most of the campaign, which lasted into early 1952. However, in January deLattre was diagnosed with cancer and died shortly thereafter.

From 1952 to 1954, the war in northern Vietnam was a stalemate. The French would attempt to extend their control into the countryside by setting up localized strong points. Some of these were overrun by the Viet Minh and some were not. The main goal of the French was to lure the Viet Minh into a large pitched battle which they were sure the Vietnamese could not win.

For two years, Giap refused to fall into the French trap. He would attack the weaker and more isolated French bases, sometimes overrunning them, sometimes not, but almost always retreating after the battle back into the highlands and jungle where the French were hesitant to follow.

At this point, both sides were locked in a stalemate. The French controlled the capital, its ports and the areas around them. The Viet Minh had control over much of the countryside. In the southern part of the country, Viet Minh influence was weaker, and though there were incessant low level attacks on French government positions, it was in the north that the war was fought.

There was one other factor working in favor of the Vietnamese: French public opinion. By 1952, the war in Vietnam had been going on for six years with more and more casualties every year. The people of France, whose economy and infrastructure was destroyed during WWII were barely getting back on their feet, and like other nations in Western Europe, was largely dependent on US Marshall Plan aid to stay afloat. One of the main problems with the war in Vietnam was its cost, which far exceeded France's current income. In addition, the France of the 1950's leaned to the left, and there was much sympathy for the Vietnamese within the country, as well as a war weariness in general. Public opinion would play a major role in the wars in Vietnam, both for the French and for the United States. General Giap knew this, and knew that to a great degree he did not have to win the war in the field he only needed to not lose it.

As part of a much larger plan to lure a sizable French force into the remote Vietnamese countryside, in 1953 Giap launched attacks against the French in the neighboring French colony of Laos. He hoped that attacks on French bases in yet another country would cause the French in Laos and in Vietnam to pursue him into the highlands where he could cut off and destroy them. This is exactly what happened over the course of 1953 and the first few months of 1954.

Near the small provincial town of Dien Bien Phu on the Vietnamese-Laotian border, overall French commander General Henri Navarre ordered a large fortification complex to be built from which operations against the Viet

Minh in both Laos and Vietnam would take place. The battle that took place at Dien Bien Phu in the spring of 1954 would change history.

Selected by the French because of its location near known Viet Minh supply routes and it production of rice, Dien Bien Phu lies in a mountain valley. In the 1950's the routes leading to other towns and supply centers were dirt and easily cut off. The French vowed to cut Vietnamese supply routes in the area, and vice versa. It was the Vietnamese who were successful.

The French at Dien Bien Phu hoped they could replicate an earlier battle at another fortified site. This fortress complex known to the French as a "hedgehog" had been cut off by the Viet Minh, but resupplied by air. Repeated Vietnamese attacks had been beaten off at high cost and the area fell largely under French control. This was the reasoning behind the French build-up at remote Dien Bien Phu. By posting an increasing number of French troops at the large complex, the French hoped that Giap would attack with an equally large Vietnamese force that could be destroyed in open battle.

The French got what they asked for, except that Giap had learned very well from his mistakes. Knowing that the Viet Minh could cut off French ground supply routes with relative ease, the Viet Minh in the area numbered over sixty thousand men, nearly fifty thousand of whom were front line soldiers, he then brought up hundreds of heavy machine guns and two dozen anti-aircraft guns recently brought in from China and the Soviet Union. French planes would not fly into Dien Bien Phu without paying a very heavy price.

The French high command, and its command on the ground in Vietnam believed that in a large conventional battle they would be victorious. The officers in command at Dien Bien Phu were believed this as well. Their opinion of the Vietnamese fighting man was not very high especially when confronted in open battle. Many, but not all, shared a similar low opinion of the Vietnamese high command. Viet Minh casualties in the Red River campaign and in many attacks on French bases since had been exceedingly high. Still, lower level officers and many of the men who had been fighting the Viet Minh felt differently.

General Giap came under criticism within his own ranks from top to bottom for the high casualties sustained by his men in both the Franco-Vietnamese and the US-Vietnamese wars. In many ways, General Giap was like American general U. S Grant during the American Civil War. He knew he could lose the men. The enemy could not. He also knew what many of his comrades did not. Many of his officers had been trained in China and later the USSR, but much of this training was relevant to revolutionary guerrilla warfare, not convention war against a well-armed and experienced enemy. The men who filled out the ranks of his army? Many times they had very little training – vigor and zeal were just as much their weapons as rifles and grenades, and the casualty rate reflected this.

Speaking of vigor and zeal since the roads and cart-paths of the low lands were either completely controlled by the French or under their guns, the only way the Viet Minh could bring in reinforcements and supplies was through the thick forests and over the mountains that surrounded the valley around the French position.

On the 13th of March 1954, Giap gave the order for the attack to begin and an extraordinarily heavy artillery bombardment rained down on the strong-points of the Dien Bien Phu position. Nearly one hundred fifty cannons, mortars and Soviet-made rocket launchers rained down on the French positions to the amazement and shock of nearly everyone there. Why a shock?

Many of the Vietnamese guns were heavy 105mm artillery pieces. Others were large 75mm guns. They had been brought into the mountains, forests and into position by hand. French command of the air and roads forced the Viet Minh to use forest trails or make them. The *smaller* 75mm guns weighed a ton and a half. Furthermore, the guns were placed in tunnels dug by hand into the back side of the mountains. The guns would fire their assigned number of rounds, then be pulled back into the mountain towards the rearward slope making them virtually impervious to French counter-battery fire. Within a week, the French officer in charge of artillery had killed himself in shame.

75mm gun being dragged into place by Viet Minh troops, Dien Bien Phu 1954

As you can see from the map on the prior page, the Vietnamese had the French virtually surrounded. The fortress complex consisted of nine strong points, given women's names alphabetically from Anne-Marie to Isabelle. The southern strong point, Isabelle, linked Dien Bien Phu to the outside world. The road south had never been under French control. All of the French supplies would have to come in by air.

There were some fifteen thousand French colonial and Foreign Legion troops at Dien Bien Phu. Frenchmen, other than officers, were not sent to Vietnam, the French government realizing that the loss of French troops in

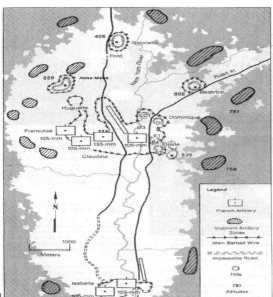

an al....., ...p.p....... .... p.., ... The colonial and Legion troops were surrounded by sixty-five thousand Vietnamese.

Before the advent of modern weapons, primarily long range rapid firing artillery and airplanes, a fortified position would be approached in a very technical and matter of fact way. Most often, this would involve the digging of a protective trench system around the fortification being attacked. This would allow the attackers to besiege the enemy with some modicum of cover, for fortresses or fortified positions were almost always surrounded by cleared open fields to allow for observation and good fields of fire. This trench work was usually done by combat engineers, known informally for many years as "sappers", a term which comes from the Latin meaning "spade". At Dien Bien Phu, the trench-digging was supervised by Viet Minh engineers, but every soldier was a "sapper".

The Viet Minh had launched diversionary attacks in the previous weeks throughout a wide area of northern Vietnam as part of their strategy at Dien Bien Phu, but the attack on the large fortified base began on March 13th. As has been mentioned, the opening Vietnamese artillery barrage came as an immense shock to the French, who were stunned both by the size and number of the Vietnamese guns which fired directly upon them from the hills surrounding the base.

The Viet Minh launched an attack on the isolated "Beatrice" outpost at dawn. Accompanied by artillery, heavy machine-gun fire, mines, grenades and much else, thousands of Viet Minh emerged from the forested hills to assault Beatrice. The thousand or so French Legionnaires were shocked by the number of the enemy coming directly at them. They rallied quickly, but French morale and effectiveness were shaken by the loss of the base commander and his staff, killed by Viet Minh artillery in the early evening. From that point on, the battle for Beatrice belonged to the Viet Minh. By midnight, the base had fallen to them. A French counter-attack the next morning was beaten back.

For the Viet Minh, the victory at Beatrice caused a great boost in morale. For the French, what normally would have been a demoralizing stroke was made that much worse by their notion that the French commanded troops were more than a match for the Vietnamese, some who went into battle in bare feet. The loss of five hundred highly trained and motivated Legionnaires also shook the French to their core.

Though the first phase of the battle was a Vietnamese victory, Giap's men had sustained greater losses than the French inside the base. This was to be expected. Generally, those attacking a fortified position can expect much greater losses than those defending. Throughout the battle, this would be the case. If battle were decided by numbers killed, the Vietnamese would have lost, but it is not. Giap knew, as he knew throughout the US war to follow, that he would sustain greater losses than his more modern enemy. He also knew that he held the dual keys to victory: the support of most of the people, and the willingness to lose as many soldiers as it took for final victory. Neither the French in the 50's nor the Americans in the 60's and 70's possessed these qualities.

The next day, Giap began the next phase of his attack. The artillery rained down on another of the French fire-bases, this one Gabrielle, on the far north of the French perimeter. Also targeted was Dien Bien Phu's airstrip. The many shell holes and the inability of the French to repair them due to Viet Minh fire put the airstrip out of action permanently.

The shelling of the airstrip was perhaps the killing stroke, though it was not apparent at the time. After the destruction of the airstrip, all French supplies now had to be dropped by parachute, and when the first supply planes came in they received a rude shock in the form of the previously unknown number of Viet Minh anti-aircraft guns. As the battle went on, two things happened: not enough supplies were being brought in to replenish what was being used (much French supply dropped into Viet Minh hands) and the wounded could not be evacuated, which further reduced French morale. Over the course of the battle, which raged until May 7th, the French lost nearly seventy planes, with over one hundred-fifty damaged. Among the losses were planes provided by the United States. Some of which were piloted by American pilots, two of whom died in action though this was kept secret for decades.

The attack on "Gabrielle" began at 5pm with an artillery barrage lasting three hours. At 8pm, with two Viet Minh regiments, approximately four thousand men, coming down through the evening under flickering parachute flare light towards the fifteen hundred or so highly trained men of the 5th Battalion/7th Algerian Rifle Regiment, the battle really began.

The Algerians fought hard and they and their comrades to the south were able to keep Gabrielle from being surrounded by keeping a route to the other bases open, but the fighting at Gabrielle was a slaughter. Casualties on the French side were about one thousand and the Viet Minh lost over that number in fighting that took place in the dark and often times hand to hand. No quarter was given on either side. A counter-attack during the night by men of French colonial Vietnamese paratroops failed with heavy losses. In the morning, the surviving Algerians and their walking wounded managed to make it back to their bases to the south.

Giap did not let up, and his next move showed him to be a very clever commander indeed. A guerrilla war is most often fought because the adversaries are not equally matched in terms of weapons, training, and manpower. Therefore, every advantage that can be gained through the use of means other than military force is utilized in guerrilla warfare.

The next French base targeted by Giap was "Anne-Marie", on the northeast of the perimeter. Mentioned at the start of this chapter is that fact that a sizable minority of the Vietnamese population is in actuality not ethnically Vietnamese. One of these groups are the Tai. This should not be mistaken for "Thai", meaning a person from nearby Thailand. Anne-Marie was defended by French led Tai troops. During the run up to the battle, Viet

Minh artillery had fired shells loaded with propaganda leaflets at Anne-Marie, which asked the Tai troops not to fight against their countrymen and to either lay down their arms and return home or join the ranks of the Viet Minh against the French. This tactic, combined with the Vietnamese victories of the last days convinced most of the Tais within the Anne-Marie perimeter to walk out of their base during the night. Some joined with the Viet Minh, many were allowed to slip through Viet Minh lines to return home. The handful of remaining Tai soldiers and French officers retreated to the main French bases to the south.

Now the Viet Minh moved to cut off the center of the French position, consisting of strong-points Dominique, Huguette, Eliane and Claudine. This would also mean that southern strong-point Isabelle, with its nearly two thousand men, would be isolated. Between Isabelle and the outside world was about two hundred miles of dirt road, mountains, and forest, all controlled by the Viet Minh. Inside Dien Bien Phu, were a number of American Chaffee tanks, which took a toll on the attackers, but these did not have the fuel to breakout to friendly territory. Moreover, the distance and the horrible narrow "roads" precluded any additional tanks being brought in from the outside.

The French at Dien Bien Phu were on their own. Everyday saw a dwindling of supply and a number of aircraft shot down by the Viet Minh AA guns in the hills. Numerous fighter aircraft attack on the hills surrounding the base did take a heavy toll, including the first use of napalm the infamous flame-producing jelly, but were unable to knock out significant numbers of the Vietnamese artillery and anti-aircraft guns hidden in caves and hillsides. A daring French infantry attack into the hills destroyed a number of Vietnamese AA guns and killed large numbers of men, but the losses in the air continued nonetheless. Airdrops were now being made at altitude, with the result that much of the French supplies were dropping into Viet Minh territory. Viet Minh loudspeakers thanked the French profusely in their own language for the gifts.

From the fall of Anne-Marie on March 17 until March 30, there was a slow-down in the fighting. The Viet Minh dug an elaborate WWI-style trench system around the base, circling ever closer. Tunnels were also dug for the movement of troops and for the placement of explosives under French positions.

The French managed to airlift out some of the wounded from the previous fighting, and bring in some supply, but not enough to replenish what had been lost and what would soon be used. Strong-points were further reinforced for the coming Viet Minh attack. Despite the losses of the other bases, and the shock of being outgunned, morale inside the French perimeter at this point was still holding, despite defeats and declining faith in the ability of their commander, Colonel Christian de Castries. He was a decorated WWII hero who now spent most of his waking hours holed up in his bunker.

On the 30th, Giap ordered a renewal in the attack. These came at the Dominique strong points, manned by Algerian infantry, mixed colonial artillery and a Foreign Legion paratroop mortar company. The strong-points of Eliane and Huguette were also assaulted.

In a series of battles that were like scenes from WWI, the French and the Vietnamese fought in and among the trenches that had been dug inside and outside the perimeter. At times the largest French guns (105mm) were set to their lowest elevation and fired nearly point blank at the Viet Minh. The Vietnamese took complete possession of some of the French positions, were then either completely or partially driven out, and then re-took some of the positions within each strong-point again.

Both sides were taking very heavy casualties, but the Vietnamese could afford it more than the French who were flying in fast fighter-bombers to assault Viet Minh positions, but could not effectively bring in reinforcements in their slow and now high-flying transport aircraft.

During the battle, General Giap proved himself able to react to the situation on the ground, but still, the heavy losses, especially those accrued in the month of April when he ordered wide spread digging and attacking from trenches and tunnels caused Viet Minh morale to plummet. Viet Minh soldiers were also angry and demoralized at the abysmal medical care available to them. Taking a cue from his heroes in the Soviet Union, Giap ordered political commissars to follow men into attacks, and shooting those who showed cowardice. He also brought in reinforcements from Laos who were not worn down from battle to enforce discipline and raise morale.

The entire month of April saw a slow grinding of the French positions, with the Vietnamese approaching ever closer to capturing all of the French strong-points which made up the Dien Bien Phu fortress complex, including the use of recently delivered Soviet "Katyusha" rocket launchers and the explosion of a large underground mine under the Eliane 2 complex, destroying it and most of its occupants.

By May 7th, Giap knew the French were on their last legs and pressed the attack. Waves of Viet Minh fighters numbering twenty-five thousand in all assaulted the last French positions, held by just three thousand weakened defenders. Many others were too ill or wounded to fight. Many others of the French force had already been captured. On the morning of May 8th, the French forces at Dien Bien Phu surrendered. Less than a hundred escaped during the night and morning to make it back to French lines in Laos. The rest, some eleven thousand entered a nightmare of captivity, which included torture. Though a few hundred were allowed to be taken out of the area by the Red Cross. Only three thousand ever made it home.

The repercussions of Giap's victory are hard to overstate. Of the countless consequences to the battle, three are perhaps most important:

1) Peace talks opened between the French and the Viet Minh *one day* after the French defeat. The conclusion of these talks was that Vietnam would be divided into two countries: North and South Vietnam, with Ho Chi Minh and the communists ruling the North and puppet emperor Bao Dai as the symbolic head of the South with the nationalist politician and former schoolmate of Giap as Prime Minister. French troops retreated south of the 17th Parallel (the area around which became known as the "Demilitarized Zone" or "DMZ"), but they pulled out after 1956. In their place a South Vietnamese national army was formed, with American advisers.

2) The United States became ever more involved in the conflict in Vietnam. The communists in the North had no intention, though they protested otherwise, of stopping their efforts at control of the northern part of the country. They also knew they were not equipped to take on France and possibly the United States in the South in the 1950's. The people of the South, different than those of the north in many ways, especially regarding free enterprise, did not support communism in the way their northern brothers did. This would take time. Ho Chi Minh and Giap, with the help of the Chinese and Soviets, would slowly build support for their cause throughout the south in the 1950's and 60's. Corrupt government in South Vietnam helped their cause.

3) For anti-colonial groups throughout Africa and Asia, the victory at Dien Bien Phu gave a huge boost to their own aspirations. The Vietnamese battle against the French was the first time in the modern era that a colonial people had defeated a modern

Western army. Throughout the 1950's and 60's, wars of independence were fought all over the world and Dien Bien Phu was the spark that ignited them.

Giap held many powerful positions during the time between the French defeat and the escalation of the war in the South with the United States: Minister of Defense, Deputy Prime Minister, Deputy Chairman of the Defense Council to Ho Chi Minh, and Commander in Chief of the People's Army. He also organized the North Vietnamese Navy and Air Force. Giap was second in power only to Ho Chi Minh, to whom he was fiercely loyal.

The only point of contention between Ho, and communist party and Giap concerned his lifestyle. While Ho was famously humble in his living habits and while the rest of the communist ruling class followed his example, Giap openly enjoyed Western food and literature, riding in a regally appointed Soviet limousine, drinking and playing the piano. His powerful position and his place within Ho's inner circle kept him safe. He had also married again, and in addition to the daughter of his first marriage, had four children with his second wife.

Though he could be in many ways "the life of the party" (no pun intended), Giap was a ruthless realist and dedicated communist. Throughout the 1950's, he led and took part in purges of Party officials, which often resulted in their deaths, and the putting down of peasant revolts against harsh communist rule in the countryside. However, unlike many of his comrades in the Communist Party, he was willing to admit mistakes, and remained popular with most of the population until his death in 2013 at age 102.

The government of South Vietnam was never viable. Too many factions vied for control. The government of Ngo Dinh Diem was pro-Western, Catholic, and authoritarian, and not much liked by the people, but he controlled the armed forces and was helped by massive amounts of Western aid, mostly from the United States. The government of the North tried on a number of occasions to assassinate Diem, but failed. It took his American "ally" to do that.

In the summer of 1963, Buddhist celebrations which turned into anti-government protests threatened the regime, and numbers of protesters were killed by government troops, who lamely tried to blame the North Vietnamese-supported "Viet Cong" guerrillas. The most enduring image from this time was a photo of a Buddhist monk setting himself on fire in public in protest against Catholic Diem's suppression of the Buddhist majority.

The self-immolation of Thich Quang Duc, one of the most famous photos of the 20th century

Events in South Vietnam soon began to spiral out of control, and the United States, concerned about the spread of communism around the world, believed that the demonstrations in South Vietnam could lead to the fall of the government and its replacement with a communist regime.

A series of botched communications in which President Kennedy's musings about the ineffectiveness of Diem's government to resolve the problems in Vietnam were taken as a green light by the US Ambassador Henry Cabot Lodge and the CIA to allow South Vietnamese army officials to capture and kill Diem and his brother and put a military run junta in their place. Both Giap and Ho Chi Minh could not believe their luck. Diem for all of his faults had proved a skilled opponent of communism in the South. Both men could scarcely believe the United States and its leadership would be so foolish as to allow Diem's killing, but they were.

The death of Diem and his replacement by an increasingly ineffective and unpopular South Vietnamese regime was accompanied by an increased North Vietnamese effort to both modernize, enlarge and equip their army, known to the West as the "NVA", and increase the strength and presence of the Viet Cong in the South.

President Kennedy had sent US military advisers to South Vietnam, most famously in the form of the new Special Forces contingent, the "Green Berets", but was wary of sending more American troops into a situation that was cloudy at best. However, not long after his assassination in November 1963, the United States and its new president, Lyndon Johnson were confronted by an incident which caused an escalation in American involvement in Vietnam and which even today is shrouded in a bit of mystery.

On August 2nd and 4th, 1964 two incidents possibly took place which propelled the United States full speed into war in Vietnam. Collectively, these incidents are called the "Gulf of Tonkin Incident" for their location off the coast of North Vietnam, but were actually two different occurrences.

Volumes have been written on the Gulf of Tonkin Incident, but for our purposes here, suffice it to say that on August 2, 1964, the United States

Navy destroyer *Maddox* which was conducting electronic intelligence operations, came under fire from North Vietnamese gunboats. The North Vietnamese claimed casualties and justified their attack by claiming that the *Maddox* had entered North Vietnamese territorial waters. The Americans adhered to a different maritime tradition which did not recognize territorial sea claims outside of twelve miles.

On the 3rd of August, President Johnson ordered the *Maddox* and another vessel to push the limits of the 12-mile boundary recognized by the United States. On the 4th, the American vessels claimed that they were under attack and fired a number of salvos at their attackers. The "attackers" were most likely radar ghosts or the other US ship. No wreckage, bodies or any evidence of Vietnamese vessels in the area was ever found and the North Vietnamese government denied the second event. Some believe that the second event was actually staged by the United States as a pretext for war, for within days the United States escalated the conflict into full-scale war, citing not only the North Vietnamese attacks on the US Navy, but its attacks throughout the South of which there was no doubt whatsoever. Thirty-one years later, US Secretary of Defense in 1964, Robert McNamara asked Giap face to face if there had ever been a second attack in the Gulf of Tonkin. Giap replied that "absolutely nothing" had happened and that the attack had been imaginary.

Nonetheless, the attacks, both real and/or imaginary caused Lyndon Johnson to propose the "Gulf of Tonkin Resolution" to Congress, which allowed the President to send all aid he deemed necessary to the nations of Southeast Asia that were under threat of communist takeover. The resolution passed, the United States immediately began to escalate its involvement in Vietnam and since its passing, and the Congress has gradually seen the erosion of its constitution right to declare war.

In a gradually escalating conflict, the United States and North Vietnam engaged each other on the ground in South Vietnam. The government of the United States not wishing to escalate the war, or cause neighboring China to become involved in the conflict as it had in Korea in the 1950's, never invaded North Vietnam. However, in the course of the war, American dropped more explosives in terms of pounds of TNT on Hanoi itself than it had in the entire European Theater in WWII.

By 1967, nearly half a million US troops were in Vietnam. For Giap, fighting the United States was both similar and different than fighting the French. Similar because he was fighting a foreign power that was both unpopular to many people, and was unfamiliar with the countryside, the people and the culture. Different because the United States, unlike France, was willing to spend the money necessary and deploy much larger forces than the French ever would or could.

Criticism of Giap and his conduct of the war has equaled the praise he received especially in the United States. Militarily, the Viet Cong and NVA lost most of the battles that it fought with the forces of the United States. Its human losses were far greater as well. This has been pointed out by many American veterans tired of hearing how they "lost the war", most notably General William Westmoreland, who commanded US forces in Vietnam in the mid-60's.

What many of these General Westmoreland and the government of the United States failed to understand was something that Vo Nguyen Giap knew from the beginning. War is does not take place only on the battlefield. It takes place in the mind and hearts of those who wage it. Giap knew that the longer the war went on, the less the American public would support it. The key for Giap and the North Vietnamese was to make the war as long and costly as possible to the United States, which was hemmed in by domestic and international opinion and action to a degree that the North Vietnamese were not.

Giap's greatest successes came because he was a great organizer more than a great tactician. One of the keys to Vietnamese success in the war was the use of the so-called "Ho Chi Minh Trail", which ran the length of the western part of the country, from north to south, and which traversed parts of Laos and Cambodia where US troops were forbidden to go. American public and political opponents of the war becoming increasingly afraid of US expansion of the war. Years of bombing at times slowed the flow of men and equipment down the Trail, but never stopped it. President Nixon ordered secret incursions into Cambodia in defiance of Congress and the wishes of the American people. The effort did nothing to stop supplies and only caused further anger in the United States.

In 1968, the NVA and Viet Cong forces besieged the Marine base at Khe Sanh in the northern central part of South Vietnam just below the DMZ. The Americans had set up the base as a place from which they could attempt to interdict supplies and NVA manpower coming south. American troops inside the base numbered over ten thousand at various times during the first six months of 1967. NVA strength was approached thirty thousand or more in the surrounding areas.

Debate has raged since 1967 about the primary purpose of the fight at Khe Sanh. Some believe that Giap was trying to re-create the battle of Dien Bien Phu. Others believe he was attempting to lure the Americans into a prolonged fight, drawing their attention elsewhere while the NVA and the Viet Cong built up their forces for a planned offensive throughout South Vietnam at the same time.

The battle at Khe Sanh raged from January to July and involved American ground, heli-borne and air forces. In the end, the Americans inflicted greater casualties by far on the Vietnamese, who slowly began to draw down their forces in the area in July. Then, almost inexplicably, the United States, which had defended Khe Sanh tooth and nail and lost upwards of three thousand killed and perhaps ten thousand wounded, including South Vietnamese forces, evacuated the area. When they did, the Viet Cong and the NVA moved back in and used the area as a staging base for the upcoming Tet Offensive.

To this day there are multiple theories about why the US forces left Khe Sanh after fighting for it for six months. Near the end of the battle, Westmoreland was replaced by WWII hero Creighton Abrams, the namesake of the Abrams tank, as US commander in Vietnam. Abrams believed that the continued use of the base was not necessary to his plans for the war, risked too much (another Dien Bien Phu), and ordered the base evacuated.

In the United States, the Tet Offensive of January which will be discussed in a moment and the evacuation of Khe Sanh after such a prolonged battle inflamed public opinion. People who had supported the war effort now began to question not only the purpose of the fighting, but the integrity of those in charge of it. Even many Marines questioned the logic of the war and the ability of the country's leaders. 1968 was the year that everything changed for the Americans in Vietnam.

Besides Khe Sanh, 1968 saw some of the greatest pitched battles of the war. This was the Tet Offensive of 1968, a military defeat for the North Vietnamese but at the same time a political victory.

Many people believe that Giap was the originator of the offensive, but this is not the case. Once the battle began, Giap had considerable input as to its direction, but he was not the sole commander of the effort. Much of that was undertaken by the Viet Cong in South Vietnam, and much of it was taken by the other North Vietnamese generals, such as Nguyen Chi Thanh.

For much of the mid-1960's the North Vietnamese government was divided in opinion and faction. This increased as leader Ho Chi Minh aged. He died in the early fall of 1969. The military was divided between those who looked to China for aid, help, and inspiration, and those who looked to the Soviet Union.

Giap was in the latter group and in the end proved victorious but in the late 1960's the Chinese group gained power. This group was in favor of all-out war in Vietnam, using both NVA and Viet Cong forces. The Soviet group had believe that a low level guerrilla war would be necessary for years perhaps even decades while the North built itself up. Members of Giap's staff were executed on trumped up charges. Giap himself was virtually untouchable, but warning was given.

The Tet Offensive began on January 30th 1968, the beginning of the Vietnamese New Year (Tet). Throughout the country Viet Cong units attacked South Vietnamese and US forces, famously including a siege of the US Embassy in Saigon, capital of the South. Every major city saw Viet Cong and NVA attacks. In Danang and Hue the fighting was some of the fiercest of the entire war. The Viet Cong went on a killing spree in some cities and towns, killing real and suspected pro-Western/pro-South Vietnamese leaders and civilians.

As was stated above, the offensive was a military defeat for the communists, and a costly one but it was a political victory. Giap and the Viet Cong had coordinated an offensive throughout an entire country which inflicted heavy casualties on American and South Vietnamese forces though far fewer than those of the North and its Viet Cong allies.

For the United States, the problem was this. The American government, both under Johnson and Nixon repeatedly assured the nation that victory in Vietnam was just around the corner. Tet proved that not only was that not true and both Johnson and Nixon knew it, but that the North and the Viet Cong had the willingness to absorb huge losses yet continue the war. Additionally, Tet illustrated that the enemy could go on the offensive *nation-wide.* They were not being defeated, and the American public and many in the military, especially in the lower and mid-level ranks knew it, as did more and more of the public and the news media.

For the next five years, the North and the US continued the war. This was marked by atrocities on both sides. The most notable being the infamous My Lai Massacre shortly after Tet in which a rogue US Army unit killed over three hundred Vietnamese civilians in cold blood.

The North Vietnamese and Viet Cong carried out terror killings on a regular basis. If a village would not cooperate with the Viet Cong, storing weapons, for example, then oftentimes the leading villagers, or sometimes the entire village would be killed as an example. BUT, for the American government and public, the massacre at My Lai and atrocities at other places only added fuel to the anti-war fire back home. American troops were "not supposed to do that", and the Vietnam War was turning many of the troops there into monsters. Public opinion of not only the war but the soldiers as well began so slip even further.

Giap knew all along that the war would be won by means other than military and he was proved right. In the early 1970's, President Richard Nixon began to draw down the number of US troops in the country, and attempt to engage the North Vietnamese at the negotiating table. At times, the North Vietnamese refused to negotiate – either because the war was going their way, or because of some point of contention between the two sides. In 1972, tiring of on again/off again talks, Nixon ordered the bombing of Hanoi and other areas of North Vietnam by not only the American naval air forces, but by the huge B-52 bombers of the US Air Force. The intense bombing, the heaviest of the war, brought the North Vietnamese back to peace talks.

While the talks went on, Giap and the North Vietnamese leadership continued the war, as did the United States, but by 1973, American forces had been reduced to their lowest level since the war began. From 1973 until 1975, the South Vietnamese would be responsible for the defense of their country, and the Americans would have, in Nixon's infamous words, "Peace with Honor", which everyone knew meant "we lost but we're acting like we didn't".

Giap knew that once the American force had been reduced to a certain point, the war would be won. The US would not send troops back to the country once it pulled out. The forces of the South Vietnamese were riddled with communist sympathizers and those who were not had poor morale, stemming from lack of faith in an incredibly corrupt government and army leadership. On April 30th, 1975, Saigon fell to the North Vietnamese. America had lost its first war and Vietnam was united. Behind most of it was Vo Nguyen Giap.

After the war, Giap had his ups and downs. He was the commander of the Vietnamese Armed Forces in the years after the war, and planned, despite opposition to the plan, the 1978 Vietnamese invasion of Cambodia whose genocidal regime had conducted cross-border raids into Vietnam. By 1978, China and Vietnam had parted ways politically over doctrinal and geo-political arguments. The Vietnamese were feeling that China, which had controlled Vietnam to varying degrees for centuries before the French, was gaining too much influence in Southeast Asia. The same year, China invaded a North Vietnamese border province as a warning, and the two fought a bloody border war which finally ended with China's withdrawal.

In the years after the war, Vietnam became a hard line communist state. Collectivization in the South entailed much suffering and many people were jailed and/or executed for real and imagined opposition to the government. Millions fled the country. Giap was side-lined in political in-fighting and chose to remain quiet despite pleas from many in the Vietnamese government to take control of the nation himself to end wide-spread abuses. He then came under criticism for not doing so, choosing to live a quiet life in retirement albeit in a large villa.

It was not until the 1990's, when Vietnam began to change after the fall of the Soviet Union and the changing of China into a more capitalist nation that Giap was rehabilitated and openly given the honors and respect he had earned in fighting for his country for forty years. When he died in 2013, he was 102, a revered figure in Vietnam and given a grudging respect in the West.

Giap in 1994 at the 40th Anniversary of the victory of Dien Bien Phu. For many Vietnamese the battle is the equivalent of the American victory at Trenton during the Revolution and Gettysburg rolled into one.

"... I think the Americans and great superpowers would do well to remember that while their power may be great, it is inevitably limited ... Since the beginning of time, whether in a socialist or a capitalist country, the things you do in the interests of the people stand you in good stead, while those which go against the interest of the people will eventually turn against you. History bears out what I say."

Vo Nguyen Giap was born in 1911 at the height of the second great wave of European Imperialism. He passed away at 102 years of age in 2013. In his lifetime, Vietnam went from a colonial backwater to a rising modern power whose military was respected around the world for its toughness and resilience. While reading these stories please note that in Vietnam, as in much of the Far East, a person's given name is written last but used as the main form of address.

Giap was born at a time when Vietnam was a nation consisting mostly of rural peasants and coastal fishermen. A number of cities lined the coast, but with the exception of two, Saigon in the south and Hanoi in the north, most Vietnamese cities were relatively small outposts dissipating slowly into the surrounding countryside. Even the Imperial city of Hue (pronounced "way") on the central coast was a small provincial city in 1911. Though the Vietnamese emperor remained on the throne, he was a symbol only – the French allowed him to remain, but without power.

For most of the world, the name "Vietnam" did not even exist. In 1911, the nation we now know as Vietnam was part of the larger French territory of French Indochina, which consisted of the modern nations of Laos, Cambodia and Vietnam.

Vietnam itself was divided into three administrative regions ranging from north to south: Tonkin, Annam and Cochin-China. Giap was born in the central region of Annam in Quang Binh province, and it was there that the formative events of his life took place.

The first was the death of his father, Vo Quang Diem. In 1919 the elder Vo was arrested by the French for subversive activity against their rule. This was likely true. Giap's father had taken part in previous uprisings against the French in the late 1880's. Held in notoriously bad conditions, Vo Quang Diem died while incarcerated.

To make matters worse, Giap's elder sister was soon arrested by the French as well. She died shortly after her release. Before he was ten years old, Giap had lost two members of his family to French maltreatment.

Giap's father had been a minor local official, and had received a formal education, which was a rarity in the Vietnam of the 19th century. Giap's education began as a young boy under his father's tutelage. After his father's death, relatives recognized Giap's intelligence and he was sent to school. This was not a common occurrence in the early 20th century either. Within two years, Giap was enrolled in a school administrated by the French in the nearest large city, the Imperial capital of Hue. The school, while under French oversight, was founded and run by a Catholic Vietnamese named Ngo Dinh Kha, and was attended by three men who would play central roles in the Vietnam of the future.

The first was Ngo Dinh Diem (1901-1963), the son of the school's founder. He would later become the President of South Vietnam and a bitter enemy of the Vietnamese communists and Giap. Diem would be South Vietnam's president until he began to lose control of the nation in 1963 amid religious and popular riots against his rule, and which were partially instigated by the North Vietnamese. Diem was assassinated by CIA operatives and replaced with another man thought to be more pliable to American wishes and aims. And another, and another...

The second of Giap's new acquaintances at the school was a young man named Pham Van Dong (1906-2000) who served as head of both North Vietnam (after the retirement of Ho Chi Minh) and the united nation of Vietnam after wars' end.

The third and most important of Giap's new acquaintances was a man named Nguyen Sinh Cung. This name was changed by tradition to Nguyen That Than ("Nguyen the Accomplished") by his proud father as a young man. Later in life when he began to publicly write and speak of Vietnamese independence, he took the name Nyugen Ai Quoc ("Nguyen the Patriot"). History knows him by his war name "Ho Chi Minh", or "He who has been enlightened", the man who led the Vietnamese independence movement against the French and much of the fight against the United States.

Giap (center) w/ Ho (center left) and Truong Trinh (later Communist Party Secretary) and Central Committee member and future diplomat Le Duc Tho (right) in 1948 during the war with France

Finding a political root in his anti-French feelings, Giap took part in protests against French rule and eventually was expelled from school for his part in the protests and his outspoken desire for Vietnamese independence. Back home after his expulsion, he joined a revolutionary movement which espoused independence and where he was introduced to communism.

In the late 1920's he returned to Hue, the center of Vietnamese political life at the time, and formed relationships with other like-minded young men and women. Giap did not join the Communist Party of Vietnam until 1931, after he had been working chaotically for independence for some time.

Though in the mind of Ho Chi Minh, who spent much of the 1920's and 30's overseas in France and the Soviet Union, communism was the model on which an independent Vietnam should be based, it should be remembered that at their core, the Vietnam Wars against the French and the United States were wars for independence and unification, with communism taking second place. There is no doubt that most of the men and women who took part in the wars were dedicated, even fanatical communists but they were Vietnamese first. This is witnessed by the subsequent war and poor relations to this day with China after the unification and the falling out with the Soviet Union in the mid-late 1980's.

In the 1930's Giap went to university in Hanoi where he studied law. He failed the equivalent of the bar exam due to the amount of time he spent in underground political activity. To earn a living, he became a history teacher. It was during this time that Giap was first truly exposed to the ideas of the military men and strategists that he would incorporate into North Vietnamese military strategy in the near future: the classic Chinese tactician and strategist Sun Tzu, Napoleon Bonaparte and the British commander who had won such fame in WWI, T.E Lawrence (better known as "Lawrence of Arabia").

During the 1930's the French regime in Indochina was a mirror of French politics at home – sometimes lenient towards left wing ideology, and sometimes not. However, by 1940 fear of both Hitler and Stalin in Europe was reflected in the French cracking down on hard-core communists at home and in their colonies after the German and Soviet dictators reached the accord of late summer 1939. Giap, Ho Chi Minh and other leading communists went into exile in China in the spring of 1940. Giap left behind a wife and child. His wife was to die in prison for revolutionary activity in 1943.

When France fell to the Germans in 1940, its far flung colonies either came under the control of the collaborationist Vichy French regime or the Free French government in exile. The colonies of Southeast Asia remained under the control of the Vichy regime, but were occupied by Germany's ally Japan in 1940. Japan allowed the Vichy French to govern the day to day affairs of the territory under Japanese direction. Now Vietnam was occupied by two foreign powers, and men like Ho Chi Minh and Giap knew from what was happening under Japanese rule in other areas that the occupation of their homeland was going to be even worse than it had been before.

Accordingly, under the leadership of Ho Chi Minh, the "Vietnamese Independence League" was formed to fight the occupation. This organization is best known by the shortening of its Vietnamese title – the "Viet Minh". Having experience in the organization of an underground political party, Giap was put in charge of organizing political activity in the China-Vietnam border area.

While in China, the Vietnamese and especially Giap, had come in contact with the Chinese communists under Mao Zedong. By 1940, the exploits of Mao and the Chinese Communist Red Army were legendary among communist revolutionaries. Having survived the thousand mile "Long March" of 1935-36, fighting and evading the forces of the Chinese Nationalists, the communists under Mao had established a large base at Yanan in central China from which they carried out a guerrilla war against the both the Nationalists and the Japanese. The tactics of the Chinese under Mao would be the model by which the Vietnamese would fight the Japanese and the French.

First they needed an army. To do this, Giap needed to return to Vietnam personally. For two years Giap and a small cadre of men worked in the mountain highlands of northern Vietnam.

One would be hard pressed to come up with a more perfect place for a hideout and base of operations than the highlands of northern Vietnam as you can see from the picture below:

Mountainous valleys like the one pictured above, river gorges, deep and thick forests and jungle in an ever changing climate that can run from hot and exceedingly humid to chilly and wet in a matter of a few hundred meters, the highlands of northern and central Vietnam were tailor-made for guerrilla war.

For those readers outside of Vietnam and Southeast Asia, it may also come as a surprise that many of the early supporters of the Viet Minh were not Vietnamese, at least not ethnically. Today, both northern and southern Vietnam is 85% ethnically Vietnamese. The other fifteen percent of the population consist of a variety of different ethnic groups and tribes, many of whom speak their own language and dialect. Many of the first people to join the Vietnamese communists under Ho and Giap were members of mountain tribes such as the Nung or Man Trang. One of the first obstacles that Giap and the others with him had to face was that of language, and initially much of the communication between the two groups was done with a primitive sign language and symbols/pictures. Communication was aided by the fact that Giap was linguistically gifted, learning French, Chinese and now the dialects of the mountain people.

Most of the first two years of their stay in the highlands was dedicated to winning over both Vietnamese and other locals to their cause, establishing an intelligence network to report on the French and Japanese, and distributing propaganda. Primitive schools were established in the highlands by the Communists, teaching local people both the basics such as reading and writing and also communist political theory and Vietnamese history.

By the summer of 1944, the Viet Minh had a wide sphere of influence in the Chinese border region and had established small cells within some of the larger villages and cities of the region. In the winter of 1944, it was decided that it was time to begin military action against the Vichy French and Japanese.

One of the first tenets of guerrilla warfare is to strike when and where it is least expected. It was decided that the first attack would take place on Christmas Day, 1944. French troops would be celebrating the holiday. They estimated that the soldiers would most likely be demoralized from being so far from home and/or drunk, and poorly trained and motivated Vietnamese colonial troops would be on duty.

Even this was risky. The Vietnamese force consisted of thirty four men and women, half of whom were armed with breech loading weapons from the late 19th century. The man who planned and led the attack was Vo Nguyen Giap.

The first Viet Minh attacks were on two small frontier outposts and were successful. Two French officers were killed and a number of Vietnamese colonial soldiers were taken prisoner and/or converted to communism. Perhaps more importantly, modern weapons and ammunition were captured as well. This was the pattern for a number of attacks that took place in winter 1944 and spring 1945. In one of these attacks, Giap was wounded in the leg, but soon recovered.

With the collapse of German resistance in France and the fall of the Vichy government, the Japanese removed all Vichy officials from what power they had left. In their place, the Japanese put the lineal Vietnamese emperor, Bao Dai (1913-1997). Bao Dai, who had been a brief college classmate of Giap, had no power and was seen during the war and afterwards to be a puppet of whatever foreign power would allow him to retain his title and way of life. First the French, then the Japanese, the French again and lastly the Americans.

With the French temporarily out of the picture the Viet Minh turned their attention to the Japanese. Though most believed the Japanese were eventually going to be defeated, no one was sure how long it would take. With this in mind, the sizable Japanese force in Vietnam remained a threat to the very end of the war. The Viet Minh, wanting their voices to be heard at any post-war international conference, began to stage hit and run attacks against the numerous Japanese outposts in the hinterlands of the country. One of their main goals was to seize as many Japanese weapons as possible, primarily artillery. In their raids, they were aided by Japan's primary enemy, the United States. This aid came in the form of small arms and officers and men from the Office of Strategic Services (the forerunner of the CIA) to train the Vietnamese in their use. This training would come back to haunt the Americans in the 1960's.

When WWII ended, the Vietnamese expected that their nation would be freed from French rule. After all, much of the rhetoric of the Allies, and of their Free French compatriot, General Charles DeGaulle, was about freedom and self-rule. However, like the Great War fought in 1914-1918, self-rule and freedom meant one thing for Europeans and entirely another for those who were not.

While Ho Chi Minh. Giap and the Viet Minh who now numbered in the thousands marched into Hanoi to form a new Vietnamese government with Ho at its head and Giap as Interior Minister, the Big Three powers met at Potsdam outside of Berlin after the end of the European war. It was there that Vietnam's fate was decided.

Joseph Stalin, Britain's new Prime Minister Clement Atlee and President Harry Truman came to the conclusion that the nation would be temporarily divided between the Nationalist Chinese under Chiang Kai-shek and the British, who would be acting on behalf of their French allies. Once the Western war ended and the French under DeGaulle had had time to re-organize, the British would hand power in Vietnam over to them.

At this point in time, the Viet Minh were in no condition to wage war against the Chinese and the British, and hoped that war-weariness and the rhetoric of freedom emanating from Western capitals would allow them to attain their goals without war.

In the time between the Japanese surrender in August and the late fall, Ho, Giap, and the Vietnamese communists had established themselves as the government in Hanoi. This brief period of self-rule was limited at best, and outside of Hanoi and the immediate area, Ho's influence was limited. By early fall tens of thousands of Nationalist Chinese and British had arrived in the north and south of the country. In late 1945, the first French troops began to arrive and the southern part of Vietnam was handed over to them by the British. The following spring, the French slowly moved into the north as well, and the Chinese began to depart.

For six months in 1946, the Vietnamese leadership was involved in talks with the French in Paris. A number of factors doomed these talks to failure. First and foremost was the French desire to regain her former position as a great power after the defeats of WWII. Another factor was Giap and measures he took within Hanoi which caused France and the Western Powers much consternation.

While Ho Chi Minh was in Paris attempting to negotiate Vietnamese independence, Giap was left in charge in Hanoi. He began to attack non-Communist Vietnamese nationalist groups in Hanoi, closing newspapers and imprisoning/killing their leaders. Rival Vietnamese factions fought each other in Hanoi's suburbs, with the communists coming out on top. More importantly, Viet Minh and the newly arriving French troops were involved in running skirmishes throughout the country.

These actions and events only fed the non-communist attitudes of Britain and the United States. In the end, France which was having its own post-war problems with communism, really never intended to allow Vietnamese independence. This was just as they refused to allow the independence of their African colonies. Giap's actions, designed to show the French that the Vietnamese had the capability to resist, doomed any chance of a peaceful settlement.

As they moved back into northern Vietnam, the French seized control of the largest port city in the country, Haiphong. The city was also key to the efforts of the Viet Minh in bringing in arms and other supplies to the north. Continual skirmishes and incidents between the French police and army and the Viet Minh escalated and in October, the local French commander took the fateful step of ordering the naval bombardment of Haiphong. This action, which caused thousands of Vietnamese casualties, made it certain that a peaceful resolution to the problems in Vietnam would not be reached. Returning from France after the fruitless talks there, Ho Chi Minh declared a state of war between the Viet Minh and France.

The first step in this war was a retreat. Giap, Ho, and the others knew that the Viet Minh were not then capable of taking on the French in Hanoi or almost anywhere else. They moved back into the northern highlands to the bases from which they fought the Japanese.

In many ways, the war known to Americans as the Vietnam War began in 1946. From the moment that Ho declared war on the French in 1946 until 1975, the northern Vietnamese and their sympathizers in the south fought continually. First against France with much American aid and then against the United States directly.

For the first two years of the Franco-Vietnamese War, the Viet Minh were limited in what they could do in their struggle. The primary problem was that of weapons and supply. Lack of weapons, not lack of manpower was the most pressing difficulty. The French had stockpiles of weapons from the war in Europe and from the United States. The Viet Minh had to rely on captured and/or smuggled weapons, both which were in limited supply.

There was one important element of war that the Viet Minh in the north did not lack, manpower. The rising world influence of the Soviet Union and in 1949 China attracted many to communism. So did Viet Minh propaganda, but the behavior of the French and the long held desire of the Vietnamese for independence provided even more. The Viet Minh spent the first two years training and conducting the same kind of small hit and run raids that were successful against the Japanese and Vichy French during WWII, and avoiding the many traps set by the French to wipe them out.

In the initial phases of the war, much of the French force consisted French colonial troops who were commanded by French officers and some non-coms, from North and Central Africa, Cambodia, and Laos. Many of the African troops were hardened veterans of the Free French campaigns in North Africa, Italy, and Europe, and had no experience as occupiers. For many of these troops, duty in Vietnam was a license for looting, rape and murder.

The one formation that consisted mostly of Europeans was the French Foreign Legion. Some of these troops were veterans of the British army who had been demobilized after the war and could find no home outside the armed forces. Many Foreign Legionnaires were Spanish fascists and a significant number were former German Wehrmacht and Waffen-SS troops. Many of the recruits had something in their past, many times a criminal history, that they wished to put behind them. Joining and surviving years in the Legion guaranteed French citizenship and a new identity. The Legion too had its share of nasty habits. These many incidents provided more recruits for the Viet Minh and fodder for communist propaganda.

The situation in Vietnam changed radically in 1949 with the victory of the Chinese Communists in their nations' civil war. With the end of war in China, the Chinese were free to provide weapons to their communist brothers to the south. Additionally, the opening of China allowed transports of weapons and supply from the Soviet Union to begin to trickle in as well.

The communist Chinese also provided advisers who helped direct and plan Viet Minh actions. Years of guerrilla warfare had made them expert, and Giap had studied both their campaigns and Mao Zedong's writing on tactics and political warfare.

By early 1950 Giap believed his forces strong enough to challenge the French in open battle. Coming down towards Hanoi from the Chinese border area, the Viet Minh inflicted a series of defeats against French forces in isolated outposts, and harassed their retreat towards Hanoi the Red River Delta area. Both sides sustained losses, but the Viet Minh gained influence over much territory and more importantly, seized stockpiles of heavy weapons and ammunition from the French outposts. This campaign took nearly a year, but when it was over, two important things had happened: much of northern Vietnam fell under Viet Minh control, and the French realized that they were in for a much bigger fight than they expected. Accordingly, they began to send sizable reinforcements to the region.

The French had retreated towards Hanoi and the Red River delta area

Vietnam - north of Hue lies the "Demilitarized Zone" (DMZ) which separated North and South Vietnam

on the Vietnamese coast. There it was easier to reinforce and resupply – and they could do this while protected by the guns of their navy. Here French fortunes began to change, temporarily.

Feeling that he had the French on the run, and controlling much of the countryside of northern Vietnam outside Hanoi, Giap, and the leadership of the Viet Minh bolstered by supplies from China, the USSR, as well as captured French weapons embarked on a series of conventional attacks at the beginning of 1951.

These attacks were a Vietnamese failure and illustrated to Giap that his forces were not ready to undertake a classic military campaign against a major power. Giap himself also learned some valuable lessons, and the seemingly careless way he threw Viet Minh forces at heavily defended French positions brought criticism on the part of some in the leadership.

In the battles of the Red River Delta, the Viet Minh lost nearly 20,000 men. The fighting took place in villages and open territory where the Vietnamese troops had little experience and the French much. Additionally, much of the fighting was against the French Foreign Legion, whose reinforced brigades were made up of heavily armed and highly motivated and trained soldiers. The French commander, General deLattre was a highly experienced and decorated WWII veteran who seemed one step ahead of Giap for most of the campaign, which lasted into early 1952. However, in January deLattre was diagnosed with cancer and died shortly thereafter.

From 1952 to 1954, the war in northern Vietnam was a stalemate. The French would attempt to extend their control into the countryside by setting up localized strong points. Some of these were overrun by the Viet Minh and some were not. The main goal of the French was to lure the Viet Minh into a large pitched battle which they were sure the Vietnamese could not win.

For two years, Giap refused to fall into the French trap. He would attack the weaker and more isolated French bases, sometimes overrunning them, sometimes not, but almost always retreating after the battle back into the highlands and jungle where the French were hesitant to follow.

At this point, both sides were locked in a stalemate. The French controlled the capital, its ports and the areas around them. The Viet Minh had control over much of the countryside. In the southern part of the country, Viet Minh influence was weaker, and though there were incessant low level attacks on French government positions, it was in the north that the war was fought.

There was one other factor working in favor of the Vietnamese: French public opinion. By 1952, the war in Vietnam had been going on for six years with more and more casualties every year. The people of France, whose economy and infrastructure was destroyed during WWII were barely getting back on their feet, and like other nations in Western Europe, was largely dependent on US Marshall Plan aid to stay afloat. One of the main problems with the war in Vietnam was its cost, which far exceeded France's current income. In addition, the France of the 1950's leaned to the left, and there was much sympathy for the Vietnamese within the country, as well as a war weariness in general. Public opinion would play a major role in the wars in Vietnam, both for the French and for the United States. General Giap knew this, and knew that to a great degree he did not have to win the war in the field he only needed to not lose it.

As part of a much larger plan to lure a sizable French force into the remote Vietnamese countryside, in 1953 Giap launched attacks against the French in the neighboring French colony of Laos. He hoped that attacks on French bases in yet another country would cause the French in Laos and in Vietnam to pursue him into the highlands where he could cut off and destroy them. This is exactly what happened over the course of 1953 and the first few months of 1954.

Near the small provincial town of Dien Bien Phu on the Vietnamese-Laotian border, overall French commander General Henri Navarre ordered a large fortification complex to be built from which operations against the Viet

Minh in both Laos and Vietnam would take place. The battle that took place at Dien Bien Phu in the spring of 1954 would change history.

Selected by the French because of its location near known Viet Minh supply routes and it production of rice, Dien Bien Phu lies in a mountain valley. In the 1950's the routes leading to other towns and supply centers were dirt and easily cut off. The French vowed to cut Vietnamese supply routes in the area, and vice versa. It was the Vietnamese who were successful.

The French at Dien Bien Phu hoped they could replicate an earlier battle at another fortified site. This fortress complex known to the French as a "hedgehog" had been cut off by the Viet Minh, but resupplied by air. Repeated Vietnamese attacks had been beaten off at high cost and the area fell largely under French control. This was the reasoning behind the French build-up at remote Dien Bien Phu. By posting an increasing number of French troops at the large complex, the French hoped that Giap would attack with an equally large Vietnamese force that could be destroyed in open battle.

The French got what they asked for, except that Giap had learned very well from his mistakes. Knowing that the Viet Minh could cut off French ground supply routes with relative ease, the Viet Minh in the area numbered over sixty thousand men, nearly fifty thousand of whom were front line soldiers, he then brought up hundreds of heavy machine guns and two dozen anti-aircraft guns recently brought in from China and the Soviet Union. French planes would not fly into Dien Bien Phu without paying a very heavy price.

The French high command, and its command on the ground in Vietnam believed that in a large conventional battle they would be victorious. The officers in command at Dien Bien Phu were believed this as well. Their opinion of the Vietnamese fighting man was not very high especially when confronted in open battle. Many, but not all, shared a similar low opinion of the Vietnamese high command. Viet Minh casualties in the Red River campaign and in many attacks on French bases since had been exceedingly high. Still, lower level officers and many of the men who had been fighting the Viet Minh felt differently.

General Giap came under criticism within his own ranks from top to bottom for the high casualties sustained by his men in both the Franco-Vietnamese and the US-Vietnamese wars. In many ways, General Giap was like American general U. S Grant during the American Civil War. He knew he could lose the men. The enemy could not. He also knew what many of his comrades did not. Many of his officers had been trained in China and later the USSR, but much of this training was relevant to revolutionary guerrilla warfare, not convention war against a well-armed and experienced enemy. The men who filled out the ranks of his army? Many times they had very little training – vigor and zeal were just as much their weapons as rifles and grenades, and the casualty rate reflected this.

Speaking of vigor and zeal since the roads and cart-paths of the low lands were either completely controlled by the French or under their guns, the only way the Viet Minh could bring in reinforcements and supplies was through the thick forests and over the mountains that surrounded the valley around the French position.

On the 13th of March 1954, Giap gave the order for the attack to begin and an extraordinarily heavy artillery bombardment rained down on the strong-points of the Dien Bien Phu position. Nearly one hundred fifty cannons, mortars and Soviet-made rocket launchers rained down on the French positions to the amazement and shock of nearly everyone there. Why a shock?

Many of the Vietnamese guns were heavy 105mm artillery pieces. Others were large 75mm guns. They had been brought into the mountains, forests and into position by hand. French command of the air and roads forced the Viet Minh to use forest trails or make them. The *smaller* 75mm guns weighed a ton and a half. Furthermore, the guns were placed in tunnels dug by hand into the back side of the mountains. The guns would fire their assigned number of rounds, then be pulled back into the mountain towards the rearward slope making them virtually impervious to French counter-battery fire. Within a week, the French officer in charge of artillery had killed himself in shame.

75mm gun being dragged into place by Viet Minh troops, Dien Bien Phu 1954

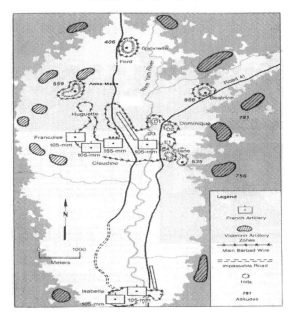

As you can see from the map on the prior page, the Vietnamese had the French virtually surrounded. The fortress complex consisted of nine strong points, given women's names alphabetically from Anne-Marie to

Isabelle. The southern strong point, Isabelle, linked Dien Bien Phu to the outside world. The road south had never been under French control. All of the French supplies would have to come in by air.

There were some fifteen thousand French colonial and Foreign Legion troops at Dien Bien Phu. Frenchmen, other than officers, were not sent to Vietnam, the French government realizing that the loss of French troops in an already unpopular war would not play well at home. The colonial and Legion troops were surrounded by sixty-five thousand Vietnamese.

Before the advent of modern weapons, primarily long range rapid firing artillery and airplanes, a fortified position would be approached in a very technical and matter of fact way. Most often, this would involve the digging of a protective trench system around the fortification being attacked. This would allow the attackers to besiege the enemy with some modicum of cover, for fortresses or fortified positions were almost always surrounded by cleared open fields to allow for observation and good fields of fire. This trench work was usually done by combat engineers, known informally for many years as "sappers", a term which comes from the Latin meaning "spade". At Dien Bien Phu, the trench-digging was supervised by Viet Minh engineers, but every soldier was a "sapper".

The Viet Minh had launched diversionary attacks in the previous weeks throughout a wide area of northern Vietnam as part of their strategy at Dien Bien Phu, but the attack on the large fortified base began on March 13th. As has been mentioned, the opening Vietnamese artillery barrage came as an immense shock to the French, who were stunned both by the size and number of the Vietnamese guns which fired directly upon them from the hills surrounding the base.

The Viet Minh launched an attack on the isolated "Beatrice" outpost at dawn. Accompanied by artillery, heavy machine-gun fire, mines, grenades and much else, thousands of Viet Minh emerged from the forested hills to assault Beatrice. The thousand or so French Legionnaires were shocked by the number of the enemy coming directly at them. They rallied quickly, but French morale and effectiveness were shaken by the loss of the base commander and his staff, killed by Viet Minh artillery in the early evening. From that point on, the battle for Beatrice belonged to the Viet Minh. By midnight, the base had fallen to them. A French counter-attack the next morning was beaten back.

For the Viet Minh, the victory at Beatrice caused a great boost in morale. For the French, what normally would have been a demoralizing stroke was made that much worse by their notion that the French commanded troops were more than a match for the Vietnamese, some who went into battle in bare feet. The loss of five hundred highly trained and motivated Legionnaires also shook the French to their core.

Though the first phase of the battle was a Vietnamese victory, Giap's men had sustained greater losses than the French inside the base. This was to be expected. Generally, those attacking a fortified position can expect much greater losses than those defending. Throughout the battle, this would be the case. If battle were decided by numbers killed, the Vietnamese would have lost, but it is not. Giap knew, as he knew throughout the US war to follow, that he would sustain greater losses than his more modern enemy. He also knew that he held the dual keys to victory: the support of most of the people, and the willingness to lose as many soldiers as it took for final victory. Neither the French in the 50's nor the Americans in the 60's and 70's possessed these qualities.

The next day, Giap began the next phase of his attack. The artillery rained down on another of the French fire-bases, this one Gabrielle, on the far north of the French perimeter. Also targeted was Dien Bien Phu's airstrip.

The many shell holes and the inability of the French to repair them due to Viet Minh fire put the airstrip out of action permanently.

The shelling of the airstrip was perhaps the killing stroke, though it was not apparent at the time. After the destruction of the airstrip, all French supplies now had to be dropped by parachute, and when the first supply planes came in they received a rude shock in the form of the previously unknown number of Viet Minh anti-aircraft guns. As the battle went on, two things happened: not enough supplies were being brought in to replenish what was being used (much French supply dropped into Viet Minh hands) and the wounded could not be evacuated, which further reduced French morale. Over the course of the battle, which raged until May 7th, the French lost nearly seventy planes, with over one hundred-fifty damaged. Among the losses were planes provided by the United States. Some of which were piloted by American pilots, two of whom died in action though this was kept secret for decades.

The attack on "Gabrielle" began at 5pm with an artillery barrage lasting three hours. At 8pm, with two Viet Minh regiments, approximately four thousand men, coming down through the evening under flickering parachute flare light towards the fifteen hundred or so highly trained men of the 5th Battalion/7th Algerian Rifle Regiment, the battle really began.

The Algerians fought hard and they and their comrades to the south were able to keep Gabrielle from being surrounded by keeping a route to the other bases open, but the fighting at Gabrielle was a slaughter. Casualties on the French side were about one thousand and the Viet Minh lost over that number in fighting that took place in the dark and often times hand to hand. No quarter was given on either side. A counter-attack during the night by men of French colonial Vietnamese paratroops failed with heavy losses. In the morning, the surviving Algerians and their walking wounded managed to make it back to their bases to the south.

Giap did not let up, and his next move showed him to be a very clever commander indeed. A guerrilla war is most often fought because the adversaries are not equally matched in terms of weapons, training, and manpower. Therefore, every advantage that can be gained through the use of means other than military force is utilized in guerrilla warfare.

The next French base targeted by Giap was "Anne-Marie", on the northeast of the perimeter. Mentioned at the start of this chapter is that fact that a sizable minority of the Vietnamese population is in actuality not ethnically Vietnamese. One of these groups are the Tai. This should not be mistaken for "Thai", meaning a person from nearby Thailand. Anne-Marie was defended by French led Tai troops. During the run up to the battle, Viet Minh artillery had fired shells loaded with propaganda leaflets at Anne-Marie, which asked the Tai troops not to fight against their countrymen and to either lay down their arms and return home or join the ranks of the Viet Minh against the French. This tactic, combined with the Vietnamese victories of the last days convinced most of the Tais within the Anne-Marie perimeter to walk out of their base during the night. Some joined with the Viet Minh, many were allowed to slip through Viet Minh lines to return home. The handful of remaining Tai soldiers and French officers retreated to the main French bases to the south.

Now the Viet Minh moved to cut off the center of the French position, consisting of strong-points Dominique, Huguette, Eliane and Claudine. This would also mean that southern strong-point Isabelle, with its nearly two thousand men, would be isolated. Between Isabelle and the outside world was about two hundred miles of dirt road, mountains, and forest, all controlled by the Viet Minh. Inside Dien Bien Phu, were a number of American Chaffee tanks, which took a toll on the attackers, but these did not have the fuel to breakout to friendly territory. Moreover, the distance and the horrible narrow "roads" precluded any additional tanks being brought in from the outside.

The French at Dien Bien Phu were on their own. Everyday saw a dwindling of supply and a number of aircraft shot down by the Viet Minh AA guns in the hills. Numerous fighter aircraft attack on the hills surrounding the base did take a heavy toll, including the first use of napalm the infamous flame-producing jelly, but were unable to knock out significant numbers of the Vietnamese artillery and anti-aircraft guns hidden in caves and hillsides. A daring French infantry attack into the hills destroyed a number of Vietnamese AA guns and killed large numbers of men, but the losses in the air continued nonetheless. Airdrops were now being made at altitude, with the result that much of the French supplies were dropping into Viet Minh territory. Viet Minh loudspeakers thanked the French profusely in their own language for the gifts.

From the fall of Anne-Marie on March 17 until March 30, there was a slow-down in the fighting. The Viet Minh dug an elaborate WWI-style trench system around the base, circling ever closer. Tunnels were also dug for the movement of troops and for the placement of explosives under French positions.

The French managed to airlift out some of the wounded from the previous fighting, and bring in some supply, but not enough to replenish what had been lost and what would soon be used. Strong-points were further reinforced for the coming Viet Minh attack. Despite the losses of the other bases, and the shock of being outgunned, morale inside the French perimeter at this point was still holding, despite defeats and declining faith in the ability of their commander, Colonel Christian de Castries. He was a decorated WWII hero who now spent most of his waking hours holed up in his bunker.

On the 30th, Giap ordered a renewal in the attack. These came at the Dominique strong points, manned by Algerian infantry, mixed colonial artillery and a Foreign Legion paratroop mortar company. The strong-points of Eliane and Huguette were also assaulted.

In a series of battles that were like scenes from WWI, the French and the Vietnamese fought in and among the trenches that had been dug inside and outside the perimeter. At times the largest French guns (105mm) were set to their lowest elevation and fired nearly point blank at the Viet Minh. The Vietnamese took complete possession of some of the French positions, were then either completely or partially driven out, and then re-took some of the positions within each strong-point again.

Both sides were taking very heavy casualties, but the Vietnamese could afford it more than the French who were flying in fast fighter-bombers to assault Viet Minh positions, but could not effectively bring in reinforcements in their slow and now high-flying transport aircraft.

During the battle, General Giap proved himself able to react to the situation on the ground, but still, the heavy losses, especially those accrued in the month of April when he ordered wide spread digging and attacking from trenches and tunnels caused Viet Minh morale to plummet. Viet Minh soldiers were also angry and demoralized at the abysmal medical care available to them. Taking a cue from his heroes in the Soviet Union, Giap ordered political commissars to follow men into attacks, and shooting those who showed cowardice. He also brought in reinforcements from Laos who were not worn down from battle to enforce discipline and raise morale.

The entire month of April saw a slow grinding of the French positions, with the Vietnamese approaching ever closer to capturing all of the French strong-points which made up the Dien Bien Phu fortress complex, including the use of recently delivered Soviet "Katyusha" rocket launchers and the explosion of a large underground mine under the Eliane 2 complex, destroying it and most of its occupants.

By May 7th, Giap knew the French were on their last legs and pressed the attack. Waves of Viet Minh fighters numbering twenty-five thousand in all assaulted the last French positions, held by just three thousand weakened defenders. Many others were too ill or wounded to fight. Many others of the French force had already been captured. On the morning of May 8th, the French forces at Dien Bien Phu surrendered. Less than a hundred escaped during the night and morning to make it back to French lines in Laos. The rest, some eleven thousand entered a nightmare of captivity, which included torture. Though a few hundred were allowed to be taken out of the area by the Red Cross. Only three thousand ever made it home.

The repercussions of Giap's victory are hard to overstate. Of the countless consequences to the battle, three are perhaps most important:

1) Peace talks opened between the French and the Viet Minh *one day* after the French defeat. The conclusion of these talks was that Vietnam would be divided into two countries: North and South Vietnam, with Ho Chi Minh and the communists ruling the North and puppet emperor Bao Dai as the symbolic head of the South with the nationalist politician and former schoolmate of Giap as Prime Minister. French troops retreated south of the 17th Parallel (the area around which became known as the "Demilitarized Zone" or "DMZ"), but they pulled out after 1956. In their place a South Vietnamese national army was formed, with American advisers.

2) The United States became ever more involved in the conflict in Vietnam. The communists in the North had no intention, though they protested otherwise, of stopping their efforts at control of

the northern part of the country. They also knew they were not equipped to take on France and possibly the United States in the South in the 1950's. The people of the South, different than those of the north in many ways, especially regarding free enterprise, did not support communism in the way their northern brothers did. This would take time. Ho Chi Minh and Giap, with the help of the Chinese and Soviets, would slowly build support for their cause throughout the south in the 1950's and 60's. Corrupt government in South Vietnam helped their cause.

3) For anti-colonial groups throughout Africa and Asia, the victory at Dien Bien Phu gave a huge boost to their own aspirations. The Vietnamese battle against the French was the first time in the modern era that a colonial people had defeated a modern Western army. Throughout the 1950's and 60's, wars of independence were fought all over the world and Dien Bien Phu was the spark that ignited them.

Giap held many powerful positions during the time between the French defeat and the escalation of the war in the South with the United States: Minister of Defense, Deputy Prime Minister, Deputy Chairman of the Defense Council to Ho Chi Minh, and Commander in Chief of the People's Army. He also organized the North Vietnamese Navy and Air Force. Giap was second in power only to Ho Chi Minh, to whom he was fiercely loyal.

The only point of contention between Ho, and communist party and Giap concerned his lifestyle. While Ho was famously humble in his living habits and while the rest of the communist ruling class followed his example, Giap openly enjoyed Western food and literature, riding in a regally appointed Soviet limousine, drinking and playing the piano. His powerful position and his place within Ho's inner circle kept him safe. He had also married again, and in addition to the daughter of his first marriage, had four children with his second wife.

Though he could be in many ways "the life of the party" (no pun intended), Giap was a ruthless realist and dedicated communist. Throughout the 1950's, he led and took part in purges of Party officials, which often resulted in their deaths, and the putting down of peasant revolts against harsh communist rule in the countryside. However, unlike many of his comrades in the Communist Party, he was willing to admit mistakes, and remained popular with most of the population until his death in 2013 at age 102.

The government of South Vietnam was never viable. Too many factions vied for control. The government of Ngo Dinh Diem was pro-Western, Catholic, and authoritarian, and not much liked by the people, but he controlled the armed forces and was helped by massive amounts of Western aid, mostly from the United States. The government of the North tried on a number of occasions to assassinate Diem, but failed. It took his American "ally" to do that.

In the summer of 1963, Buddhist celebrations which turned into anti-government protests threatened the regime, and numbers of protesters were killed by government troops, who lamely tried to blame the North Vietnamese-supported "Viet Cong" guerrillas. The most enduring image from this time was a photo of a Buddhist monk setting himself on fire in public in protest against Catholic Diem's suppression of the Buddhist majority.

The self-immolation of Thich Quang Duc, one of the most famous photos of the 20th century

Events in South Vietnam soon began to spiral out of control, and the United States, concerned about the spread of communism around the world, believed that the demonstrations in South Vietnam could lead to the fall of the government and its replacement with a communist regime.

A series of botched communications in which President Kennedy's musings about the ineffectiveness of Diem's government to resolve the problems in Vietnam were taken as a green light by the US Ambassador Henry Cabot Lodge and the CIA to allow South Vietnamese army officials to capture and kill Diem and his brother and put a military run junta in their place. Both Giap and Ho Chi Minh could not believe their luck. Diem for all of his faults had proved a skilled opponent of communism in the South. Both men could scarcely believe the United States and its leadership would be so foolish as to allow Diem's killing, but they were.

The death of Diem and his replacement by an increasingly ineffective and unpopular South Vietnamese regime was accompanied by an increased North Vietnamese effort to both modernize, enlarge and equip their army, known to the West as the "NVA", and increase the strength and presence of the Viet Cong in the South.

President Kennedy had sent US military advisers to South Vietnam, most famously in the form of the new Special Forces contingent, the "Green Berets", but was wary of sending more American troops into a situation that was cloudy at best. However, not long after his assassination in November 1963, the United States and its new president, Lyndon Johnson were confronted by an incident which caused an escalation in American involvement in Vietnam and which even today is shrouded in a bit of mystery.

On August 2nd and 4th, 1964 two incidents possibly took place which propelled the United States full speed into war in Vietnam. Collectively, these incidents are called the "Gulf of Tonkin Incident" for their location off the coast of North Vietnam, but were actually two different occurrences.

Volumes have been written on the Gulf of Tonkin Incident, but for our purposes here, suffice it to say that on August 2, 1964, the United States Navy destroyer *Maddox* which was conducting electronic intelligence operations, came under fire from North Vietnamese gunboats. The North Vietnamese claimed casualties and justified their attack by claiming that the *Maddox* had entered North Vietnamese territorial waters. The Americans adhered to a different maritime tradition which did not recognize territorial sea claims outside of twelve miles.

On the 3rd of August, President Johnson ordered the *Maddox* and another vessel to push the limits of the 12-mile boundary recognized by the United States. On the 4th, the American vessels claimed that they were under attack and fired a number of salvos at their attackers. The "attackers" were most likely radar ghosts or the other US ship. No wreckage, bodies or any evidence of Vietnamese vessels in the area was ever found and the

North Vietnamese government denied the second event. Some believe that the second event was actually staged by the United States as a pretext for war, for within days the United States escalated the conflict into full-scale war, citing not only the North Vietnamese attacks on the US Navy, but its attacks throughout the South of which there was no doubt whatsoever. Thirty-one years later, US Secretary of Defense in 1964, Robert McNamara asked Giap face to face if there had ever been a second attack in the Gulf of Tonkin. Giap replied that "absolutely nothing" had happened and that the attack had been imaginary.

Nonetheless, the attacks, both real and/or imaginary caused Lyndon Johnson to propose the "Gulf of Tonkin Resolution" to Congress, which allowed the President to send all aid he deemed necessary to the nations of Southeast Asia that were under threat of communist takeover. The resolution passed, the United States immediately began to escalate its involvement in Vietnam and since its passing, and the Congress has gradually seen the erosion of its constitution right to declare war.

In a gradually escalating conflict, the United States and North Vietnam engaged each other on the ground in South Vietnam. The government of the United States not wishing to escalate the war, or cause neighboring China to become involved in the conflict as it had in Korea in the 1950's, never invaded North Vietnam. However, in the course of the war, American dropped more explosives in terms of pounds of TNT on Hanoi itself than it had in the entire European Theater in WWII.

By 1967, nearly half a million US troops were in Vietnam. For Giap, fighting the United States was both similar and different than fighting the French. Similar because he was fighting a foreign power that was both unpopular to many people, and was unfamiliar with the countryside, the people and the culture. Different because the United States, unlike France, was willing to spend the money necessary and deploy much larger forces than the French ever would or could.

Criticism of Giap and his conduct of the war has equaled the praise he received especially in the United States. Militarily, the Viet Cong and NVA lost most of the battles that it fought with the forces of the United States. Its human losses were far greater as well. This has been pointed out by many American veterans tired of hearing how they "lost the war", most notably General William Westmoreland, who commanded US forces in Vietnam in the mid-60's.

What many of these General Westmoreland and the government of the United States failed to understand was something that Vo Nguyen Giap knew from the beginning. War is does not take place only on the battlefield. It takes place in the mind and hearts of those who wage it. Giap knew that the longer the war went on, the less the American public would support it. The key for Giap and the North Vietnamese was to make the war as long and costly as possible to the United States, which was hemmed in by domestic and international opinion and action to a degree that the North Vietnamese were not.

Giap's greatest successes came because he was a great organizer more than a great tactician. One of the keys to Vietnamese success in the war was the use of the so-called "Ho Chi Minh Trail", which ran the length of the western part of the country, from north to south, and which traversed parts of Laos and Cambodia where US troops were forbidden to go. American public and political opponents of the war becoming increasingly afraid of US expansion of the war. Years of bombing at times slowed the flow of men and equipment down the Trail, but never stopped it. President Nixon ordered secret incursions into Cambodia in defiance of Congress and the wishes of the American people. The effort did nothing to stop supplies and only caused further anger in the United States.

In 1968, the NVA and Viet Cong forces besieged the Marine base at Khe Sanh in the northern central part of South Vietnam just below the DMZ. The Americans had set up the base as a place from which they could attempt to interdict supplies and NVA manpower coming south. American troops inside the base numbered over ten thousand at various times during the first six months of 1967. NVA strength was approached thirty thousand or more in the surrounding areas.

Debate has raged since 1967 about the primary purpose of the fight at Khe Sanh. Some believe that Giap was trying to re-create the battle of Dien Bien Phu. Others believe he was attempting to lure the Americans into a prolonged fight, drawing their attention elsewhere while the NVA and the Viet Cong built up their forces for a planned offensive throughout South Vietnam at the same time.

The battle at Khe Sanh raged from January to July and involved American ground, heli-borne and air forces. In the end, the Americans inflicted greater casualties by far on the Vietnamese, who slowly began to draw down their forces in the area in July. Then, almost inexplicably, the United States, which had defended Khe Sanh tooth and nail and lost upwards of three thousand killed and perhaps ten thousand wounded, including South Vietnamese forces, evacuated the area. When they did, the Viet Cong and the NVA moved back in and used the area as a staging base for the upcoming Tet Offensive.

To this day there are multiple theories about why the US forces left Khe Sanh after fighting for it for six months. Near the end of the battle, Westmoreland was replaced by WWII hero Creighton Abrams, the namesake of the Abrams tank, as US commander in Vietnam. Abrams believed that the continued use of the base was not necessary to his plans for the war, risked too much (another Dien Bien Phu), and ordered the base evacuated.

In the United States, the Tet Offensive of January which will be discussed in a moment and the evacuation of Khe Sanh after such a prolonged battle inflamed public opinion. People who had supported the war effort now began to question not only the purpose of the fighting, but the integrity of those in charge of it. Even many Marines questioned the logic of the war and the ability of the country's leaders. 1968 was the year that everything changed for the Americans in Vietnam.

Besides Khe Sanh, 1968 saw some of the greatest pitched battles of the war. This was the Tet Offensive of 1968, a military defeat for the North Vietnamese but at the same time a political victory.

Many people believe that Giap was the originator of the offensive, but this is not the case. Once the battle began, Giap had considerable input as to its direction, but he was not the sole commander of the effort. Much of that was undertaken by the Viet Cong in South Vietnam, and much of it was taken by the other North Vietnamese generals, such as Nguyen Chi Thanh.

For much of the mid-1960's the North Vietnamese government was divided in opinion and faction. This increased as leader Ho Chi Minh aged. He died in the early fall of 1969. The military was divided between those who looked to China for aid, help, and inspiration, and those who looked to the Soviet Union.

Giap was in the latter group and in the end proved victorious but in the late 1960's the Chinese group gained power. This group was in favor of all-out war in Vietnam, using both NVA and Viet Cong forces. The Soviet group had believe that a low level guerrilla war would be necessary for years perhaps even decades while the North built itself up. Members of Giap's staff were executed on trumped up charges. Giap himself was virtually untouchable, but warning was given.

The Tet Offensive began on January 30th 1968, the beginning of the Vietnamese New Year (Tet). Throughout the country Viet Cong units attacked South Vietnamese and US forces, famously including a siege of the US Embassy in Saigon, capital of the South. Every major city saw Viet Cong and NVA attacks. In Danang and Hue the fighting was some of the fiercest of the entire war. The Viet Cong went on a killing spree in some cities and towns, killing real and suspected pro-Western/pro-South Vietnamese leaders and civilians.

As was stated above, the offensive was a military defeat for the communists, and a costly one but it was a political victory. Giap and the Viet Cong had coordinated an offensive throughout an entire country which inflicted heavy casualties on American and South Vietnamese forces though far fewer than those of the North and its Viet Cong allies.

For the United States, the problem was this. The American government, both under Johnson and Nixon repeatedly assured the nation that victory in Vietnam was just around the corner. Tet proved that not only was that not true and both Johnson and Nixon knew it, but that the North and the Viet Cong had the willingness to absorb huge losses yet continue the war. Additionally, Tet illustrated that the enemy could go on the offensive *nation-wide.* They were not being defeated, and the American public and many in the military, especially in the lower and mid-level ranks knew it, as did more and more of the public and the news media.

For the next five years, the North and the US continued the war. This was marked by atrocities on both sides. The most notable being the infamous My Lai Massacre shortly after Tet in which a rogue US Army unit killed over three hundred Vietnamese civilians in cold blood.

The North Vietnamese and Viet Cong carried out terror killings on a regular basis. If a village would not cooperate with the Viet Cong, storing weapons, for example, then oftentimes the leading villagers, or sometimes the entire village would be killed as an example. BUT, for the American government and public, the massacre at My Lai and atrocities at other places only added fuel to the anti-war fire back home. American troops were "not supposed to do that", and the Vietnam War was turning many of the troops there into monsters. Public opinion of not only the war but the soldiers as well began so slip even further.

Giap knew all along that the war would be won by means other than military and he was proved right. In the early 1970's, President Richard Nixon began to draw down the number of US troops in the country, and attempt to engage the North Vietnamese at the negotiating table. At times, the North Vietnamese refused to negotiate – either because the war was going their way, or because of some point of contention between the two sides. In 1972, tiring of on again/off again talks, Nixon ordered the bombing of Hanoi and other areas of North Vietnam by not only the American naval air forces, but by the huge B-52 bombers of the US Air Force. The intense bombing, the heaviest of the war, brought the North Vietnamese back to peace talks.

While the talks went on, Giap and the North Vietnamese leadership continued the war, as did the United States, but by 1973, American forces had been reduced to their lowest level since the war began. From 1973 until 1975, the South Vietnamese would be responsible for the defense of their country, and the Americans would have, in Nixon's infamous words, "Peace with Honor", which everyone knew meant "we lost but we're acting like we didn't".

Giap knew that once the American force had been reduced to a certain point, the war would be won. The US would not send troops back to the country once it pulled out. The forces of the South Vietnamese were riddled with communist sympathizers and those who were not had poor morale, stemming from lack of faith in an incredibly corrupt government and army leadership. On April 30th, 1975, Saigon fell to the North Vietnamese. America had lost its first war and Vietnam was united. Behind most of it was Vo Nguyen Giap.

After the war, Giap had his ups and downs. He was the commander of the Vietnamese Armed Forces in the years after the war, and planned, despite opposition to the plan, the 1978 Vietnamese invasion of Cambodia whose genocidal regime had conducted cross-border raids into Vietnam. By 1978, China and Vietnam had parted ways politically over doctrinal and geo-political arguments. The Vietnamese were feeling that China, which had controlled Vietnam to varying degrees for centuries before the French, was gaining too much influence in Southeast Asia. The same year, China invaded a North Vietnamese border province as a warning, and the two fought a bloody border war which finally ended with China's withdrawal.

In the years after the war, Vietnam became a hard line communist state. Collectivization in the South entailed much suffering and many people were jailed and/or executed for real and imagined opposition to the government. Millions fled the country. Giap was side-lined in political in-fighting and chose to remain quiet despite pleas from many in the Vietnamese government to take control of the nation himself to end wide-spread abuses. He then came under criticism for not doing so, choosing to live a quiet life in retirement albeit in a large villa.

It was not until the 1990's, when Vietnam began to change after the fall of the Soviet Union and the changing of China into a more capitalist nation that Giap was rehabilitated and openly given the honors and respect he had earned in fighting for his country for forty years. When he died in 2013, he was 102, a revered figure in Vietnam and given a grudging respect in the West.

Giap in 1994 at the 40th Anniversary of the victory of Dien Bien Phu. For many Vietnamese the battle is the equivalent of the American victory at Trenton during the Revolution and Gettysburg rolled into one.

"... *I think the Americans and great superpowers would do well to remember that while their power may be great, it is inevitably limited ... Since the beginning of time, whether in a socialist or a capitalist country, the things you do in the interests of the people stand you in good stead, while those which go against the interest of the people will eventually turn against you. History bears out what I say.*"

Chapter 11: "Charlie"

"Victor Charlie", the American term for the Viet Cong using letters of the military alphabet. Even more common were "VC" or "Charlie". In this war of increasing frustration, Americans of all backgrounds also used the now offensive terms "Gooks", "Zips" and much else.

Behind all of this terminology was a perverse respect. For many American GI's and Marines, the Viet Cong and the NVA were an enemy to be respected and sometimes feared. Most prolonged engagements with the Viet Cong and the NVA ended with an American tactical victory yet, in the end the VC and NVA achieved their aim.

One of the main problems in engaging the VC was in determining exactly who they were. Infiltrating and recruiting in villages throughout the South, the Viet Cong were made up of men, women, and teenagers. They were farmers, workers, cab drivers, waiters...the list went on. One thing that many Viet Cong were not was uniformed. As another generation of Americans were to find out in Iraq in the 2000's, one of the primary problems in fighting a guerrilla war is figuring out who your enemy is and where they are.

The Americans tried a policy of "search and destroy", spreading out throughout the country constantly patrolling throughout the countryside looking for VC/NVA bases of operations, weapons caches, and headquarters. Many times these operations were "successful". Weapons were captured, some VC may have been killed, and plans/documents found. The problem was that it seemed that for every VC killed, three more took their place, more weapons were brought in and the plans in the documents immediately changed.

Many times, however, "search and destroy" operations were efforts in futility. A village from which VC activity was reported was calm and no evidence found, or perhaps the village was empty. Sometimes Marines or GI's would walk into a village and find many of its inhabitants dead. They had refused to cooperate with the VC. Whatever the case, it frequently seemed as if the US was fighting ghosts. By the time the Americans got to a hamlet, the VC were long gone.

"Fortified hamlets" were tried. Villages from the countryside would be forcibly evacuated by the Americans or their South Vietnamese allies, and the villagers gathered in areas that were supposed to be sealed. This was thought to keep the VC out. Virtually never did. Sometimes villagers would be VC sympathizers. The forcible evacuation of their centuries' old homes by the Americans caused many villagers to think of the VC as defenders, or at least as the lesser of two evils. The infiltration of the villages went on regardless. Sometimes villagers had relatives in the VC and the ARVN ("Army of the Republic of Vietnam") at the same time. In a world almost completely alien to them in language, culture, custom and environment, Americans in Vietnam often felt as if they were fighting on another planet. "Back to the world" was a phrase often used by Americans to describe the end of their tour of duty and their return home.

Who were the VC? Many if not most were dedicated communists. Historians in the West have debated for years as to whether communist ideals or Vietnamese patriotism was the prime motivating factor among the Viet Cong. Since the Vietnamese break with China in the late 1970's, differences with the Soviet Union/Russia in the late 1980's and 1990's, many have seen the Vietnam War as more of a patriotic conflict than an ideological one. Accordingly, the primary motivation behind those in the Viet Cong may not have a desire to establish a communist utopia in Vietnam, but for the freedom to decide for themselves what type of government they wanted without foreign interference. Though the communists were not big on freedom of decision.

While some Viet Cong operated in small cells in cities throughout the country, gathering intelligence, etc., many others were in the countryside forming combat units and fighting the Americans and South Vietnamese for control of the nation.

In the jungles, highlands, and rice paddies that were native to them, the Viet Cong fought mainly hit and run battles against their enemies, striking quickly at a specific target and then vanishing back into the cover of the forest. Covering their tracks and protecting them were a variety of defensive systems that gave the Americans nightmares.

The Viet Cong had no air-power. No planes. No helicopters. The North Vietnamese had an air force, but this was devoted to defending Hanoi and the North from massive American attacks. With no air-power and very little air defense, the Viet Cong was forced to improvise and they were masters at it.

Talk to American combat veterans and they will tell you stories of mines made from wood and planted on the raised roads running through rice paddies and then being ambushed when they slogged through the knee or waist deep water.

*Pfc. Lacey Skinner of Alabama moves through the mud of a rice paddy
while under fire in 1966 (courtesy of telegraph.co.uk)*

The Viet Cong were also infamous for their booby traps, the two most well-known were covered holes or pits which a GI could fall into, landing on bamboo stakes covered in human or water buffalo excrement to infect the wounded man, who usually was pierced through the foot or leg.

These "punji sticks" could also be passed through clay or tied in such a way as to make a large spiked ball or board which could be rigged to a snare. "Toe-popper" mines, consisting of a bullet or small shell placed above a nail and buried in the ground could take someone's foot off. Wounding a man not only took him out of the fight, but the three or four of his comrades that it took to care for him or remove him from the battlefield.

Grenades placed in the forest or underwater in rice paddies whose firing pin was pulled by a GI or innocent farmer or ox walking through also was a common VC weapon. The number of booby traps in Vietnam was astounding. They were also cheap, which was especially important to the VC whose access to weapons, though good, was limited. The toll they took on the American psyche and morale cannot be measured. Oftentimes, a booby trap placed in June might go off in July, August or months later or even years. When it did, the Americans had no one to fight against. The VC who placed it was long, long gone.

Another important factor was the terrain. As was mentioned in the first chapter, the Vietnamese countryside, especially away from the coast, was tailor made for guerrilla war. Thick jungle, rice paddies, swamps, mountains, and mountainous forests, river deltas – almost all of which were unfamiliar to most Americans, even those from rural areas. It is sometimes said that GI's and Marines from Louisiana were more able to adjust to the landscape of Vietnam than others, the Bayou State resembling in both heat and vegetation that of Southeast Asia.

Though it existed at the time, night vision technology was limited in number and not of very good quality. The overwhelming number of American troops in Vietnam never saw a piece of it. Therefore, US troops in Vietnam were most active during the day when their overwhelming firepower could most effectively be brought to bear.

That meant that in large part, the movement of the Viet Cong and NVA within South Vietnam took place at night. Years after the war, singer Billy Joel wrote an ode to American Vietnam veterans titled "Goodnight Saigon", one line of which is appropriate to quote here: "We held the day in the palm of our hands. They ruled the night, and the night – seemed to last as long as six weeks on Parris Island" (the Marine Corps basic training camp).

During the siege of Dien Bien Phu in the 50's and at Khe Sanh and other places in the 60's, the Viet Minh/Viet Cong learned that their frequent night attacks had a demoralizing effect on the enemy. Throughout the American involvement in Vietnam, a pattern was established: the Americans would make forays into the countryside during the day, investigating villages and reports of enemy activity, returning to base or establishing strong-points at night – a sort of "circle the wagons" mentality. During the night, the enemy would frequently return, replace found booby traps, move weapons stores in danger of being found, and live to fight another day under more advantageous circumstances.

One of the most frustrating of Viet Cong tactics was the used of tunnel systems to avoid American air-power and observation, storage, headquarters and barracks. The most famous of these were the tunnel systems at Chu-Chi, which were perhaps the most elaborate. The diagram on the next page shows a typical VC tunnel complex.

As you can see these tunnel systems, the overwhelming majority of which were dug by hand, were simple and complex at the same time. In addition to allowing the VC to remain concealed, they provided medical care and command/control. One of the most frustrating (for the Americans/South Vietnamese) aspects of the tunnel systems was that they allowed the Viet Cong to remain undercover until the enemy had passed by. Reports by American officers in the field would indicate no enemy presence and a day later other American troops, believing the area to be clear, might be ambushed. These ambushes frequently took place from the rear, further demoralizing the enemy.

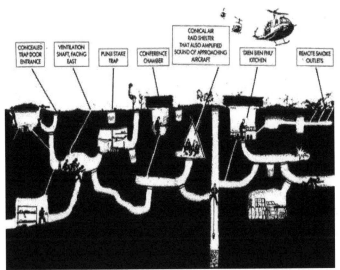

The Americans found many, but not all of the tunnels. Dogs, sound detection equipment and simple careful observation worked many times. Once the tunnels were found, however, more problems could begin.

Most, but not all of the time, the VC would know American troops had found their tunnel complexes. A system of sentries, alarms and booby traps would tell them so. That meant that most times, the Americans found abandoned tunnels.

Though VC lives might have been saved, this was still a blow. Many hours, days and weeks of labor had been wasted. Evacuation frequently happened at the last moment, so many times supplies and weapons were lost.

The Americans employed a number of tactics to destroy or clear the tunnels, but the most famous were the "tunnel rats". Many of these volunteers were miners from states like West Virginia who would go in to investigate, usually armed with only a .45 pistol and a flashlight. Being a tunnel rat required nerves of steel and a small body to maneuver through the narrow dark passages.

After investigation and perhaps skirmishes underground, US forces would use explosives to seal or destroy the tunnels. Many times napalm was dropped from the air- upon explosion, the jellied liquid bursting into flame and pouring into every opening possible.

The heavy foliage in Vietnam was also used to great effect by the Viet Cong, especially to cover their movements along the Ho Chi Minh Trail. To counter this, US planes began to drop a defoliant, code-named "Agent Orange" on wide swathes of the countryside, denuding it of trees. American troops would sometimes be on the ground, exposed to Agent Orange, or ordered into areas recently sprayed. Years later, many Vietnam veterans succumbed to, or are suffering from, the many ailments (primarily forms of cancer) caused by Agent Orange.

Considering the overwhelming firepower and technology at the disposal of US forces, how was it that the Viet Cong continued to fight and eventually win? Let's briefly examine the life of a Viet Cong member and see if that helps us round out the picture. An L.A Times article from 2006 can help us gain insight into a previously unknown enemy.

One of the biggest Vietnamese bestsellers in the mid-2000's was a sort of Vietnamese equivalent of the diary kept by Anne Frank during WWII. It is an unvarnished peek into the life of a young Vietnamese woman who joined the Viet Cong and served as a surgeon and nurse in the front lines for three years. It is also one of the first published accounts of life in the Viet Cong. Many veterans did not talk much about their experiences, and committing something to the page can be a dangerous thing if those in power do not like what they read.

The Vietnamese government has recently relaxed some of its controls on speech and the written word, and the society has opened up in general, accepting much of the same capitalist spirit that has engulfed China. In a Vietnam increasingly populated with those who have no experience of the war, and whose concerns with worldly goods sometimes vexes those in power, the words of a long dead patriot are useful, not a danger.

Much to the amazement of many readers, the diary also contains passages critical of the communist leadership. She speaks of being discriminated against because of her upper-middle class background, and her resistance to being controlled by party members whose petty bickering upset her greatly.

The diary was found and taken home by an American intelligence officer in 1970. In the early 2000's, he donated the diary to the Vietnam Center at Texas Tech University. The experts there tracked down the surgeon's mother in Vietnam and gave her copies of the diary. This has been published in Vietnam, selling four hundred thousand copies. A book is a best seller in Vietnam if it sells five thousand.

The Viet Cong surgeon/nurse was named Dang Thuy Tram, and her diary conveys the same longings, sadness and frustration as Anne Frank's diary of the 1940's: "Sadness soaks into my heart just like the long days of rain soak into the earth...Oh! Why was I born a girl so rich with dreams, love, and asking so much from life?"

Unlike Anne's diary, Tram's diary includes patriotism: "I will perish for the country, tomorrow's victory song will not include me ... I am one of those people who give their blood and bones in order to take back the country. But what is so special about that? Millions and millions of people like me have fallen already yet have never enjoyed one happy day, so I am never sorry."

For many Americans, both at home and in Vietnam, the enemy was a mysterious quantity: foreign, alien and difficult to fathom, especially in the face of military defeat after defeat. Of course, those fighting a war have demonized their enemies since time began, but to many Americans, the Vietnamese were almost non-human - "gooks" who did not know when to give up.

Fortunately, times of peace tend to heal many wounds. Not all, sadly, but many, and since the end of the war, many Americans (both veterans and tourists) have gone to Vietnam and been warmly welcomed. The officer who found Tram's diary is one of those.

Still, Tram did not live to see days of peace. She was separated from the man she loved by the war, and watched many Viet Cong soldiers die right before her eyes. Her views on the Americans of the 1960's were clear, as in this passage about her separation from the love of her life: "With those pirates robbing our country, every time I think about you [dying] my heart is so filled with hate I cannot breathe. We must force them to pay for their crimes."

Throughout most of her time at war, Tram worked at rudimentary field hospitals near the northern South Vietnamese coastal city of Duc Pho. Like Viet Cong everywhere in South Vietnam, Tram and her comrades frequently had to move and rebuild elsewhere, or when they Americans bombed or destroyed their hospital and left, simply build it again.

Tram was a dedicated communist as well as a patriot and envisioned the death she was sure would come to her. She remembers starring in school musicals and then imagines her funeral: "Now I am also an actor on the stage of life: I am playing a girl of the Liberation with a black dress, every night following the guerrillas in their activities in our area close to the enemy ... Maybe I will meet the enemy, and maybe I will fall with my hand carrying the red-crossed box, and then people will also feel sorry for the girl sacrificed to the Revolution during her dream-filled youth."

The last entry for her diary was June 20, 1970. She was killed in an American attack on June 22. An American veteran who was there later told the intelligence officer (whose name is Frederic Whitehurst) that he saw the doctor try to fend off the Americans with an old French rifle. She was killed by a single bullet to her forehead.

One of her last entries reads "Oh, life changed by blood and bones, by the youth of so many people, how many lives have ended in order to allow other lives to be fresh and green?"

Conclusion

Until 2011, the Vietnam War had been the longest conflict in American history. That has now been superseded by the US involvement in Afghanistan that began shortly after the attacks of 9/11.

Some fifty-five thousand Americans lost their lives in Vietnam, and countless veterans and their families have suffered and still suffer long after the conflict. Homelessness, poverty, drug use, and the effects of secret government programs like the experimental defoliant "Agent Orange"...the list goes on.

For the Vietnamese, the war lasted decades. Hundreds of thousands died in the ten year war against the French. Vietnamese estimates of its combat dead in the conflict against the United States is just over a million. American Defense Department estimates run from half a million Vietnamese combat deaths to over nine hundred thousand. Tens of thousands were killed in Laos and Cambodia, and a similar number died due to unexploded ordnance and mines in the years after the war.

The lowest estimates of Vietnamese, in both South and North, is over one million. The highest, over three. Unexploded ordnance and exposure to chemical agents still kills Vietnamese every year. American vets are still suffering from exposure as well.

The United States was not the same country after Vietnam. This is when the so-called "Generation Gap" of understanding between the young and the older generation of WWII truly began. Much of the counter-culture of the time centered on protest against Vietnam and what people on both sides believe it stood for. There is both good and bad to be said about the events that occurred in the United States as a result of the war – but those change depending on who you speak with.

In 21st century dollars, the war cost the American public over one trillion dollars. It took the Vietnamese decades to rebuild their nation and establish a modern economy.

When the last US combat troops were withdrawn from Vietnam in 1973, President Nixon called it "Peace with Honor". No one believed it then, and no one believes it now. Vietnam was America's first significant military defeat, and the blow to the armed forces of the country took years to heal. It perhaps did not heal until the victory over Iraq in 1990-1991. What has happened since is a matter for the historians of the future.

Some older Americans and some Vietnam veterans will say that the war was not "lost" by the military. The numbers would back that up. The Vietnamese, in both the northern and southern parts of the country, suffered horrible losses.

The Vietnam War was a paradox in many ways, the primary one being that from many points of view, the war was "won" by the United States – at least on the battlefield, but as we have since learned, the battlefield is not the only place where was is waged.

Another paradox for you to consider: during the war, the Vietnamese were supported by the People's Republic of China and the Soviet Union. Both nations sent advisers, weapons, and other supplies to the country. Both nations lost a number of those advisers in combat or as a result of American bombing.

In 1978, the Vietnamese fought a short but very intense ground war against the Chinese, as was mentioned earlier. After that conflict, relations between the USSR and Vietnam became much closer, the USSR and China at the time being enemies.

In the late 1980's and early 1990's as the Soviet Union fell apart, relations between the two countries worsened, which led to the Vietnamese ordering the Soviet Navy to leave the port of Cam Ranh Bay, which they used for much of their Pacific fleet.

At the same time, the Vietnamese and the United States slowly engaged each other in a series of agreements. For example, the Vietnamese allowed the US to search for American remains in the country. In exchange, the US spent millions of dollars in a clean-up effort in Vietnam, attempting to rid the country of its left-over ordnance.

In the late 2000's Vietnam and Russia have established a working relationship, but it is not nearly as close as it had been at one time. China and Vietnam are rivals – a series of territorial disputes in the waters off Vietnam have kept relations tense.

Of the three superpowers, in 2015 it is the United States which enjoys the closest relationship with the Vietnamese government and nation.

In conclusion, there is a famous dictum – a quote – by the famous German (Prussian) strategist von Clausewitz: "War is politics by other means." The opposite sometimes holds true. Politics is war by other means. One cannot, especially in the 20th and 21st centuries, separate politics from war. If we could, then the Vietnam War would not have nearly torn America apart. Vietnam was an American defeat.

However, that should be not understood, by civilians or veterans to mean that the sacrifices of those who died in Vietnam were unnoticed and their heroism unremembered. It has not been, as you have just read.

Finally, we would like to ask you to give a short, honest, and unbiased review of this book.

Click HERE to leave a Review.

Please & Thank you!

Check Out My Other Books

Below you'll find some of my other popular books that are listed on Amazon and Kindle as well. Simply click on the links below to check them out. Alternatively, you can click on my author name here ->"Ryan Jenkins" on Amazon to see other work done by me.

- Irma Grese & Other Infamous SS Female Guards
- World War 2: A Brief History of the European Theatre
- World War 2 Pacific Theatre: A Brief History of the Pacific Theatre
- World War 2 Nazi Germany: The Secrets of Nazi Germany in World War II
- The Third Reich: The Rise & Fall of Hitler's Germany in World War 2
- World War 2 Soldier Stories: The Untold Stories of the Soldiers on the Battlefields of WWII
- World War 2 Soldier Stories Part II: More Untold Tales of the Soldiers on the Battlefields of WWII
- Surviving the Holocaust: The Tales of Survivors and Victims
- World War 2 Heroes: Medal of Honor Recipients in WWII & Their Heroic Stories of Bravery
- World War 2 Heroes: WWII UK's SAS hero Robert Blair "Paddy" Mayne
- World War 2 Heroes: Jean Moulin & the French Resistance Forces
- World War 2 Snipers: WWII Famous Snipers & Sniper Battles Revealed
- World War 2 Spies & Espionage: The Secret Missions of Spies & Espionage in WWII
- World War 2 Air Battles: The Famous Air Combat that Defined WWII
- World War 2 Tank Battles: The Famous Tank Battles that Defined WWII
- World War 2 Famous Battles: D-Day and the Invasion of Normandy
- World War 2 Submarine Stores: True Stories from the Underwater Battlegrounds
- The Holocaust Saviors: True Stories of Rescuers who risked all to Save Holocaust Refugees
- Irma Grese & The Holocaust: The Secrets of the Blonde Beast of Auschwitz Exposed

- Auschwitz & the Holocaust: Eyewitness Accounts from Auschwitz Prisoners & Survivors
- World War 2 Sailor Stories: Tales from Our Warriors at Sea
- World War 2 Soldier Stories Part III: The Untold Stories of German Soldiers
- World War 2 Navy SEALs: True Stories from the First Navy SEALs: The Amphibious Scout & Raiders

If these links do not work for whatever reason, you can simply search for these titles on the Amazon website to find them.

Instant Access to Free Book Package!

As a thank you for the purchase of this book, I want to offer you some more material. We collaborate with multiple other authors specializing in various fields. We have best-selling, master writers in history, biographies, DIY projects, home improvement, arts & crafts and much more! **We make a promise to you to deliver at least 4 books a week in different genres, a value of $20-30, for FREE!**

All you need to do is sign up your email here at http://nextstopsuccess.net/freebooks/ to join our Book Club. You will get weekly notification for more free books, courtesy of the First Class Book Club.

As a special thank you, we don't want you to wait until next week for these 4 free books. We want to give you 4 **RIGHT NOW**.

Here's what you will be getting:

1. A fitness book called "BOSU Workout Routine Made Easy!"
2. A book on Jim Rohn, a master life coach: "The Best of Jim Rohn: Lessons for Life Changing Success"
3. A detailed biography on Conan O'Brien, a favorite late night TV show host.
4. A World War 2 Best Selling box set (2 books in 1!): "The Third Reich: Nazi Rise & Fall + World War 2: The Untold Secrets of Nazi Germany".

To get instant access to this free ebook package (a value of $25), and weekly free material, all you need to do is click the link below:

http://nextstopsuccess.net/freebooks/

Add us on Facebook: First Class Book Club

64723481R00104

Made in the USA
Middletown, DE
17 February 2018